Leonard Lindsay

Exhibition of early Italian art from 1300 to 1550 at the New Gallery

Leonard Lindsay

Exhibition of early Italian art from 1300 to 1550 at the New Gallery

ISBN/EAN: 9783742885166

Manufactured in Europe, USA, Canada, Australia, Japa

Cover: Foto ©Thomas Meinert / pixelio.de

Manufactured and distributed by brebook publishing software
(www.brebook.com)

Leonard Lindsay

Exhibition of early Italian art from 1300 to 1550 at the New Gallery

EXHIBITION

OF

Early Italian Art

From **1300** *to* **1550.**

The New Gallery,

REGENT STREET.

1893-4.

Arrangement of the Exhibition.

SOUTH GALLERY.
PICTURES AND ILLUMINATED MANUSCRIPTS.

WEST GALLERY.
PICTURES, CHURCH PLATE, BRONZES, JEWELLERY, WOOD-CARVINGS
AND PLAQUES.

NORTH GALLERY.
PICTURES, DRAWINGS, IVORIES, MAJOLICA, BRONZES, MUSICAL
INSTRUMENTS AND MEDALS.

CENTRAL HALL.
MAJOLICA, ARMOUR, EMBROIDERIES AND FURNITURE.

BALCONY.
PRINTED BOOKS, AUTOGRAPH LETTERS, DRAWINGS, &C.

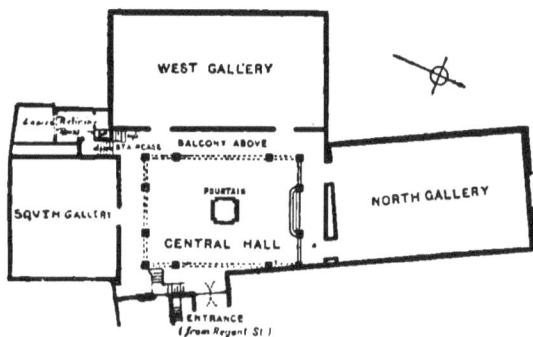

2384

THE GENERAL COMMITTEE.

President:

THE EARL OF CARLISLE.

PREFATORY NOTE.

The Directors of the New Gallery and the Secretary desire to tender their most grateful thanks to Lord Carlisle and the members of the Committee for the assistance they have afforded in organising the present Exhibition, and for the valuable contributions, which they and other ladies and gentlemen have made of pictures, bronzes and other works of art.

They also wish to record their deep sense of obligation to those who have taken a more active part in the practical organisation of the Exhibition ; in particular to Mr. Grueber and Mr. Isidore Spielman, for their arduous labours in the arrangement of the various exhibits and in the preparation of the catalogue ; and to Mr. Sidney Colvin, Mr. Fairfax Murray, Dr. Richter, Mr. C. H. Read, Mr. Lionel Cust, Mr. Everard Green, Mr. Laking Mr. R. R. Holmes, Mr. Cockerell, Mr. Charles Davis, Mr. St. John Hope, and Mr. Jenner, for the advice and assistance they have given in the selection of the various exhibits. '

Prefatory Note.

The Directors of the New Gallery hope next winter to complete the illustration of early Italian art by an Exhibition of the arts of Venice, Padua, Verona, Bologna and Ferrara, cities which have not been represented on the present occasion.

LEONARD C. LINDSAY,
Secretary.

NOTE ON THE ARRANGEMENT OF THE EXHIBITION.—*Although no strictly chronological order has been attempted in the placing of the pictures, an endeavour has been made to group together artists of the same period and of the same cities: but in some instances, owing to the exigencies of the hanging this has not been adhered to. The Committee have also considered that it would make the section of the Printed Books more interesting if works printed in Venice were included in the present Exhibition. In the case of works of art other than pictures the period has been extended to the end of the 16th Century.*

CATALOGUE.

The Numbers commence in the South Gallery and continue from left to right.

₊ *Throughout the Catalogue, in describing the pictures, the* RIGHT *and the* LEFT *mean those of the spectator facing the picture.*

The works are catalogued under the names given to them by the Contributors. The Committee cannot be responsible in all cases for the attributions.

SOUTH GALLERY.

FIRST ROOM.

MASTERS OF THE XIII.—XIV. CENTURIES.

1. VIRGIN AND CHILD.

> Full-length figure of the Virgin seated to right, holding the Infant Saviour on her knees; He holds an ear of millet in right hand and small bird in left; gold background. Panel, arched top, 44 × 27 in.

By GIOVANNI DA PISA.   Lent by MRS. BLOOD.

2. TRIPTYCH.

> On the centre panel, lower half, are the Virgin and Child between two female Saints, to one of whom Christ offers a branch of lilies; above and on the two wings are depicted scenes from the life of Christ. Centre Panel 29 × 20½ in. Wings 29 × 9½ in. each.

By GIOTTO.   Lent by A. E. STREET, ESQ.

B

3. St. Catherine of Siena Delivering the Rule to the Sisters of the Second Order of St. Dominic.

In the centre St. Catherine seated on a throne between two pots of lilies, and trampling on Satan, delivers with her right hand a book to six nuns kneeling before her, and with her left receives a charter of foundation from a widow lady attended by another lady and two other nuns; in the background St. Lawrence, St. Dominic, St. Peter Martyr, and St. Raphael with Tobias and the dog. Fresco painting. Panel 62½ × 62½ in.

By Cosimo Roselli.   Lent by Charles Butler, Esq.

4. The Assumption of the Virgin.

In the centre full-length figure of the Virgin within a mandorla supported by a crowd of angels; she holds in her hands the girdle which she is in the act of presenting to St. Thomas, who is seen in half-length below. Panel, circular, 25 in.

By Filippo di Dalmasio.   Lent by Charles Butler, Esq.

5. Virgin and Child.

Small full-length figure of the Virgin, seated to left on a cushion feeding the Infant Jesus, who is dressed in yellow; above four angels, two of whom hold a crown; gold background. Panel 30 × 20 in.

By Agnolo Gaddi.   Lent by Charles Butler, Esq.

6. Virgin and Child.

Small three-quarter length figure of the Virgin holding the Infant Saviour; gold background. Panel 23 × 10 in.

By Cimabue.   Lent by Charles Butler, Esq.

7. Triptych.

In the centre panel the Virgin seated, facing, holding the Infant Christ; above, a circle of angels, the Holy Ghost and God the Father; on the left wing St. Antony, St. John the Baptist, and four other Saints; on the right wing the Crucifixion with the Virgin and St. John; above on the points of the wings the Annunciation; gold background. Panel 28½ × 24 in.

School of Giotto.   Lent by Henry Wagner, Esq.

8. The Virgin and Child Enthroned.

In the centre the Virgin enthroned holding the Infant Saviour; before on the left are St. Bartholomew and St. Benedict, and on the right St. Peter and St. Francis of Assisi; behind the throne on the left stand St. Ursula and St. Stephen, and on the right St. Apollonia and St. Catherine. Panel 26½ × 13 in.

Early Florentine School.   Lent by Charles Butler, Esq.

9. THREE APOSTLES.

Small half-length figures of St. Peter, St. Bartholomew and St. John. Panel 7 × 14 in.

By BENOZZO GOZZOLI.   Lent by the EARL OF CRAWFORD, K.T.

10. THREE APOSTLES.

Small half-length figures of St. Paul, St. Philip, and St. James the Greater. Panel 7 × 14 in.

By BENOZZO GOZZOLI.   Lent by the EARL OF CRAWFORD, K.T.

11. MARTYRDOM OF SS. COSMO AND DAMIAN.

In two compartments; on the left one SS. Cosmo and Damian, crucified, are being stoned and shot at with arrows by soldiers and others; in the background three Saints in prayer; on the right panel SS. Cosmo and Damian being beheaded. Panel 18 × 17 in. each.

By BARTOLO DI FREDI.   Lent by CHARLES BUTLER, ESQ.

12. ST. ANTHONY.

Half-length figure of the Saint to right, holding a book in left hand; right resting on crutch; gold background. Panel 31 × 12½ in.

FLORENTINE SCHOOL.   Lent by HENRY WILLETT, ESQ.

13. VIRGIN AND CHILD WITH ST. JOHN THE BAPTIST AND ST. MICHAEL.

Half-length figure of the Virgin standing to front with the Infant Christ seated on her right arm; behind on the right St. Michael, and on the left St. John the Baptist; gold background. Panel 22½ × 16 in.

By MATTEO DA SIENA.   Lent by HENRY WILLETT, ESQ.

14. ST. BERNARD.

Small full-length figure of the Saint, seated facing on a throne in the act of blessing; and holding book with left hand; below are monks kneeling; above on either side, angels. Panel 10 × 10 in.

EARLY FLORENTINE SCHOOL.   Lent by A. E. STREET, ESQ.

15. THE TRIUMPH OF CHASTITY.

Car to left drawn by two unicorns; on the car Chastity enthroned holding open book; before her, Love bound, his wings held by two winged boys; procession of Virgins; landscape background with buildings. Panel 16½ × 48 in. From the Barker Collection.

FLORENTINE SCHOOL.   Lent by LORD WANTAGE, V.C.

B 2

---

16. CORONATION OF THE VIRGIN.

Full-length seated figures ; Christ on the right in red robe and blue mantle is placing the crown on the head of the Virgin, who in attitude of adoration wears white robes edged with black ; gold background. Panel, arched, 43 × 27 in.

By GIOTTO.   Lent by CONSTANTINE IONIDES, ESQ.

17. TWO SCENES FROM THE LIFE OF ST. JOHN THE BAPTIST.

(1) Birth of St. John. Within a room, Elizabeth lying in a bed ; in the centre foreground, St. John held by an attendant ; on the right, Zacharias seated writing on a scroll ; on the left a woman warming clothes at a fire ; on the floor, basin and ewer. (2) St. John departing to the wilderness. Small figure of the saint issuing from a building on the left and another similar figure of him in the centre ascending a rocky pass. Panel (1) 11½ × 14½ in. ; (2) 11½ in. × 19 in. (See also No. 18.)

By GIOVANNI DI PAOLO DA SIENA.   Lent by CHARLES BUTLER, ESQ.

18. TWO SCENES FROM THE LIFE OF ST. JOHN THE BAPTIST.

(1) Baptism of Christ. Small figures of the Saviour in the water and St. John on the brink in the act of baptising Him ; the Father represented in the clouds ; and other figures. (2) Head of St. John the Baptist brought in on a charger. Small figures of Herod and two other persons at a table ; the head presented by a kneeling page ; the daughter of Herodias and two others standing by. Panels (1) 11½ × 17 in. (2) 11½ × 14 in. (See also No. 17.)

By GIOVANNI DI PAOLO DA SIENA.   Lent by CHARLES BUTLER, ESQ.

19. VIRGIN AND CHILD WITH ANGELS.

Half-length figure of the Virgin holding the Infant Christ, supported by two angels ; in a glory. Panel 11½ × 8¼ in.

By FILIPPINO LIPPI.   Lent by MRS. HENRY GORDON.

20. VIRGIN AND CHILD WITH SAINTS.

Small full-length figure of the Virgin seated on throne holding the Infant Saviour erect on her knees ; on the left stand St. John the Baptist, St. Nicholas and St. Agnes, and on the right St. Catherine, St. Anthony and St. Bartholomew ; two angels in the background. Panel, arched, 18 × 10 in.

SCHOOL OF GIOTTO.   Lent by MRS. BLOOD.

21. THE CRUCIFIXION.

Christ on the Cross between the two thieves ; six angels hover around ; at the foot of the Cross, the fainting Virgin, supported by the two Marys ; behind them St. John and St. Mary Magdalen, her hands raised to the crucified Saviour; on the right are soldiers; gold background. Panel 24 × 15 in.

From the Collections of M. DE BAMMEVILLE and Rev. WALTER DAVENPORT BROMLEY.

By DUCCIO DI BUONINSEGNA.   Lent by the EARL OF CRAWFORD, K.T.

22. THE SACRIFICE OF IPHIGENIA.

In the centre a burning altar; on the right stands Iphigenia accompanied by one female and two male attendants, one of whom is pointing to a stag feeding; on the right stands Agamemnon in attitude of despair, and near him are attendants, one youth is holding two horses; above in clouds Diana; on the left, in the background, ships. Panel 10 × 19 in.

By GIOVANNI CAROTO.   Lent by CHARLES BUTLER, ESQ.

23. THE ASSUMPTION OF THE VIRGIN.

Full-length figure of the Virgin seated in glory within a mandorla, supported by six angels; below is the empty tomb with flowers, in front of which kneel St. Bonaventura and St. Francis in attitudes of adoration; mountainous background. Panel 76 × 56 in.

By FRA ANGELICO.   Lent by WILLIAM FULLER MAITLAND, ESQ.

24. THE PRESENTATION IN THE TEMPLE.

In the centre a marble canopy on four columns above an altar on the right of which leans Simeon with the Infant Christ in his arms; behind him stands Anna, holding a scroll, and on the left the Virgin Mary, with St. Joseph; gold background. Panel 17½ × 17 in.

BY GIOTTO.   Lent by HENRY WILLETT, ESQ.

25. THE VIRGIN AND CHILD WITH ST. MARK AND ST. JOHN THE BAPTIST.

Three compartments; in the centre the Virgin seated full-length with the Infant Christ on her knees; on the left stands St. Mark holding a book, and on the right St. John the Baptist with a scroll; gold background. Panel 13 × 23 in.

By BERNA DA SIENA.   Lent by HENRY WAGNER, ESQ.

26. THE DESCENT FROM THE CROSS.

In the centre the cross with St. Joseph of Arimathea and St. John, who are lowering the body of Christ into the arms of the Virgin, behind whom are the three Holy Women; another apostle is extracting the nail from the Saviour's feet; gold background. Panel 15½ × 21 in. (See also No. 67). From the Fuller-Russell Collection.

By UGOLINO DA SIENA.   Lent by HENRY WAGNER, ESQ.

27. FOUR SAINTS.

Small full-length figures of a Bishop, a Cardinal, and two Saints of the Order of Mount Carmel in separate compartments, under arches.   Panel 15½ × 21½ in.

By MASACCIO.   Lent by CHARLES BUTLER, ESQ.

28. "NOLI ME TANGERE."

Small full-length figure of Christ holding hoe in left hand and extending His right towards St. Mary Magdalen, who kneels on the left.   Panel 21 × 14 in.

By TADDEO GADDI.   Lent by HENRY WAGNER, ESQ.

29. THE ANNUNCIATION.

In a room on the right kneels the Virgin ; before her St. Gabriel ; on the left doorway through which is seen landscape.   Panel 7 × 13½ in.

By FRA ANGELICO.   Lent by CHARLES BUTLER, ESQ.

30. THE CRUCIFIXION AND THE PIETÀ. (DIPTYCH.)

On the left panel, the Christ crucified ; on either side of the Cross stand the Holy Women and St. John, and soldiers.   On the right panel, the dead Christ being placed in the tomb by the Holy Women and St. John ; behind stand St. Joseph of Arimathea, and others ; in the distance, the cross, hills, &c. ; gold background. Panel 15½ × 10½ in. each.

Two more panels, part of the same series, are in the Bargello, at Florence.

By AMBROGIO LORENZETTI.

31. THE CORONATION OF THE VIRGIN.

In clouds, the Virgin crowned by Christ ; in foreground below are St. Barbara and St. Ursula kneeling ; behind them St. Augustine and St. Julian ; at foot Christ rising from the tomb ; to left St. Francis ; to right St. Nicholas of Tolentino. Panel, circular top, 36 × 17 in.   From the Rogers Collection.

By LORENZO DI CREDI.   Lent by LORD WANTAGE, V.C.

32. VIRGIN AND CHILD ENTHRONED.

Small full-length figure of the Virgin, seated facing on throne, holding the Infant Saviour ; around are saints and angels playing musical instruments ; gold background.   Panel 23 × 11½ in.

By BERNARDO DADDI.   Lent by CHARLES BUTLER, ESQ.

33. ST. PETER RESTORING TABITHA.

Small full-length figures ; Tabitha, seated on a couch to right, raises her hands to St. Peter, who is in the act of blessing ; on the left a man and a woman in attitudes of surprise ; on the right a disciple. Panel 10 × 8¾ in.

By SANO DI PIETRO DA SIENA.   Lent by WILLIAM FULLER MAITLAND, ESQ.

34. SAINTS IN ADORATION.

Small full-length figures of saints kneeling to right ; on the left St. Catherine of Siena, holding a heart ; gold background. Panel 11¾ × 9¾ in. Part of a predella.

By BARTOLO DI FREDI.   Lent by MRS. BLOOD.

35. ST. GEORGE.

Under life-size full-length figure of the saint, in corset and green and red robe, grasping a banner in his right hand and resting left hand on a shield. Panel, circular top, 49¾ × 21½ in.

By LORENZO DI CREDI.   Lent by the EARL OF ROSEBERY, K.G.

36. THE TRIUMPH OF LOVE AND CHASTITY.

Landscape ; in the foreground are two processions, each with a triumphal car, one representing the Triumph of Love, the other the Triumph of Chastity. Panel 16 × 55½ in.

By DELLO DELLI.   Lent by the MARQUESS OF LOTHIAN, K.T.

37. THE MIRACLE OF ST. NICHOLAS.

Before the Saint, on the left, are three tubs, in each of which is standing the nude figure of a child ; behind him kneel a man and a woman ; in the right background is a man engaged in pouring some liquid into a jar. Panel 12 × 22 in.

This picture is intended to represent the miracle said to have been performed by St. Nicholas at Myra during the famine. Whilst travelling through his diocese he lodged in the house of a man who stole little children, then murdered them and served up their limbs as food for his guests. Such a repast he laid before the bishop, who was immediately aware of the fraud, and going to the tubs where the remains of the slaughtered children were salted down, made over them the sign of the cross, and they were restored to life and stood up.

FLORENTINE SCHOOL.   Lent by CHARLES BUTLER, ESQ.

---

38. VIRGIN AND CHILD.

Small three-quarter length figure of the Virgin seated to left holding the Infant Christ on her knees ; above on the left open window.   Panel 19½ × 14 in.

By SANDRO BOTTICELLI.   Lent by the REV. W. H. WAYNE.

39. THE CORONATION OF THE VIRGIN.

Small three-quarter length figures ; Christ seated to left is placing a crown on the Virgin's head, who is in attitude of devotion ; above and around are cherubim and seraphim ; gold background.   Panel, octagonal, 22 × 16½ in.

By ANDREA ORCAGNA.   Lent by SIR WILLIAM FARRER.

40. THE CRUCIFIXION.

The Christ crucified ; at the foot of the cross are the Virgin and St. John ; from the cross grows a tree on which rests a pelican feeding her young.   Panel 38½ × 18½ in.

By CENNINO CENNINI.   Lent by CHARLES BUTLER, ESQ.

41. THE ENTOMBMENT OF THE VIRGIN.

The body of the Virgin lowered into the tomb by two angels ; two others hold torches ; towards the right, figure of Christ, surrounded by angels, holding the soul of the Virgin in His arms ; the Apostles stand behind.   Panel 39½ × 35 in.

UMBRIAN SCHOOL.   Lent by CHARLES BUTLER, ESQ.

42. TWO SCENES FROM THE LIFE OF CHRIST.

No. 1.—THE CALL OF ST. PETER AND ST. ANDREW. ("Follow me and I will make you fishers of men.")   Christ standing to right on the sea-shore is addressing St. Peter and St. Andrew, who are in a boat, their fishing net in the water ; gold background.

No. 2.—THE RAISING OF LAZARUS. ("Lazarus, come forth.")   Christ with his disciples and others standing before the tomb of Lazarus ; before him kneels Mary the sister of Lazarus and near her stands her sister Martha ; at the entrance of the tomb, which is hewn out of a rock, is seen the shrouded body of Lazarus ; gold background.   Panel 17 × 17½ in. each.

These with No. 56 form part of an altar-piece similar to the large one now in the Opera del Duomo at Siena.

By DUCCIO DI BUONINSEGNA.

43. VIRGIN AND CHILD.

Full-length figure of the Virgin seated, facing, on an architectural throne, and holding the Infant Saviour erect upon her knees ; behind are five angels, four of whom hold branches of lilies ; in the foreground on either side are angels playing musical instruments ; between them a vase of flowers.   Panel 53½ × 34½ in.

By BENOZZO GOZZOLI.   Lent by HENRY WAGNER, ESQ.

44. VIRGIN AND CHILD.

Half-length figure of the Virgin in adoration over the Infant Christ, Who lies before her; at His feet a pomegranate. Panel 21¼ × 16 in.

By ALESSIO BALDOVINETTI. Lent by J. ANNAN BRYCE, ESQ.

45. THE CORONATION OF THE VIRGIN (ALTAR PIECE).

In the centre Christ and the Virgin seated on a Gothic throne ; He places a conical-shaped crown on her head ; before them five angels kneeling and playing musical instruments ; on the left full-length figures of St. Lawrence and St. Stephen, and on the right similar figures of St. John the Baptist and St. John the Evangelist ; all within an ornamented Gothic frame decorated on the left with figures of St. Bartholomew, St. Francis and St. Silvester, and on the right St. Anthony, St. Dominic, and St. Proculus, and angels ; below a dedicatory inscription with the date 1408. Panel 51½ × 82½ in.

FLORENTINE SCHOOL.

Lent by the RECTOR OF THE ITALIAN CHURCH, HATTON GARDEN.

46. THE CRUCIFIXION.

Christ on the Cross ; the Magdalen kneeling at the foot ; on the left the Holy Women and the Virgin swooning ; on the right the centurion pointing to the Saviour and addressing spectators to right. Panel 14 × 8 in.

By GIOTTINO. Lent by HENRY WAGNER, ESQ.

47. THE CRUCIFIXION.

Christ crucified ; at the foot of the cross is St. Mary Magdalen ; to the right the Virgin and St. John ; to the left St. Christopher and St. Nicholas ; gold background. Panel 15½ × 10½ in.

By CENNINO CENNINI. Lent by CHARLES BUTLER, ESQ.

48. THE DEATH OF THE VIRGIN.

The Virgin lies on a 'couch with the Apostles behind her, and St. Peter, wearing cope and tiara, and holding the aspersory ; above, in a mandorla, surrounded by angels, half-length figure of Christ holding the soul of the Virgin on His left arm ; in the foreground two women seated reading. Architectural frame. Panel 13 × 7½ in.

By TADDEO GADDI. Lent by ISAAC FALCKE, ESQ.

49. VIRGIN AND CHILD.

Half-length figure of the Virgin seated, facing, the Infant Saviour on her left arm ; she is holding in her right hand the model of a church ; behind are two angels holding scrolls with inscriptions ; gold background. Panel 23 × 17½ in.

By MATTEO DA SIENA. Lent by CHARLES BUTLER, ESQ.

50. THE ADORATION OF THE MAGI.

On the left the Virgin seated in a shed, the Infant Saviour on her knees ; before her, the three Magi ; St. Joseph in the background ; architectural frame.   Panel 13 × 7½ in.

By TADDEO GADDI.   Lent by ISAAC FALCKE, ESQ.

51. VIRGIN AND CHILD.

Small three-quarter-length figure of the Virgin seated, facing, on a cushion and holding the Infant Child, Who stands on her knees ; on either side two angels ; two others hold a crown over her head ; gold background ; arched gold frame.   Panel 9½ × 8 in.

By TADDEO DI BARTOLO.   Lent by HENRY WAGNER, ESQ.

52. THE CORONATION OF THE VIRGIN.

Small full-length figure of Christ seated on throne crowning the Virgin, who kneels before Him ; around are angels, some playing musical instruments ; gothic frame. Panel 12½ × 9¼ in.   From the Fuller-Russell Collection.

By TADDEO GADDI.   Lent by HENRY WAGNER, ESQ.

53. THE VIRGIN AND POPE LEO IX.

Half-length figure of the Virgin standing to left, both hands raised in prayer ; above on left is the small half figure of the First Person of the Holy Trinity ; in front of a balustrade underneath is seen the half-length figure of Pope Leo, his right hand miraculously cured by an angel ; his left raised in thanksgiving. Along the balustrade is the following inscription : " Imago coram qua orando Leo Papa sensit sebi manum restitutam " ; gold background.   Panel 44 × 30 in.

It is related that the hand of Pope Leo IX. having been kissed by a woman withered. Through the intercession of the Virgin Mary an angel was sent from heaven who touched the withered hand and it was instantly cured.

FLORENTINE SCHOOL.   Lent by CHARLES BUTLER, ESQ.

54. VIRGIN AND CHILD.

Half-length figure of the Virgin seated to the front with the Infant Saviour erect on her knees ; in the background St. Jerome and St. Mary Magdalen.   Panel 24½ × 17½ in.

By MATTEO DA SIENA.   Lent by S. SCROPE, ESQ.

55. VIRGIN AND CHILD WITH SAINTS.

Half-length figure of the Virgin facing, before a parapet, on which stands the Infant Saviour, His right hand raised in benediction; behind them are figures of St. Sebastian and St. Nicholas; landscape background.   Panel 35 × 27½ in.

By MATTEO DA SIENA.   Lent by HENRY WAGNER, ESQ.

56. TWO SCENES FROM THE LIFE OF CHRIST.

No. 1.—CHRIST AND THE WOMAN OF SAMARIA.   ("I that speak unto thee am He.") Christ seated to right on the well head is addressing the woman of Samaria, who stands in the centre of the picture, a pitcher on her head, and in her left hand a water-pot; her right hand is raised; on the right is the gateway of the city in which stand four men; gold background.

No. 2.—THE TEMPTATION.   ("Get thee behind me, Satan.") Christ facing standing on the Mount, reproving Satan, who points out to Him "all the kingdoms of the world" represented by cities; on the right are the two ministering angels; gold background.   Panel 17 × 17½ in. each.   (See also No. 42.)

By DUCCIO DI BUONINSEGNA.

57. VIRGIN AND CHILD ENTHRONED.

Small full-length figure of the Virgin seated, facing, head to left, holding the Infant Saviour; on the steps of the throne sit and stand four angels playing harp, viols, and cymbals; gold background.   Panel 31 × 22 in.

By DOMENICO BARTOLI DA SIENA.   Lent by CHARLES BUTLER, ESQ.

58. VIRGIN AND CHILD WITH ANGELS.

Full-length figure of the Virgin seated on a throne, facing, holding the Infant Christ erect upon her knees; in front, two angels playing musical instruments.   Panel 36 × 21½ in.

By SIMONE MEMMI.   Lent by S. SCROPE, ESQ.

59. THE STORY OF JOSEPH.

On the left Jacob blessing Joseph; towards the centre Joseph's brethren selling him to the Ishmaelites in the desert; on the right, within a colonnaded building, Joseph fleeing from Potiphar's wife; Joseph interpreting Pharaoh's dreams, and Joseph in . prison.   Panel 17 × 64½ in.   (See also No. 77.)

By PESELLINO.   Lent by C. BRINSLEY MARLAY, ESQ.

60. BATTLE SCENE.

Battle scene; combat of cavalry in the foreground; in the background on the right a soldier presenting a head on a salver to a seated general; and to the left a fortified town. A scene from Roman history, possibly the defeat and death of Crassus. Panel 16 × 54 in.

Probably the front of a cassone.

FLORENTINE SCHOOL.   Lent by the EARL OF CRAWFORD, K.T.

61. THE MARRIAGE OF THE VIRGIN.

Small full-length figures ; within the Temple, in the centre, stands Zacharias, facing, holding the right hands of the Virgin and St. Joseph, who, about to put the ring on the Virgin's finger, holds in his left hand a staff on the top of which is a dove ; on the right are female attendants, on the left male attendants, some of whom are blowing trumpets. Panel 8 × 23½ in.

By FRA ANGELICO.   Lent by CHARLES BUTLER, ESQ.

62. TRIPTYCH.

In the centre, the Virgin and Child ; on the wings, St. Michael and St. Nicholas ; gold stamped background. Panel 24 × 2½ in.

FLORENTINE SCHOOL.   Lent by CHARLES BUTLER, ESQ.

63. THE NATIVITY.

The Infant Christ lying in the manger and raising His hands to the Virgin kneeling in adoration ; on the left St. John ; in the background the ox and the ass. Panel 18 × 16 in.

By SANDRO BOTTICELLI.   Lent by WILLIAM FULLER MAITLAND, ESQ.

64. VIRGIN AND CHILD WITH ANGELS.

Half-length seated figure of the Virgin, facing, holding the Child on her lap, Who holds a sprig of narcissus in His right hand ; on the left an angel holding a glass with other sprigs of narcissus, and on the right another angel adoring. Panel 25 × 18 in.

Lent by the EARL OF ASHBURNHAM.

By BENVENUTO DA SIENA, formerly ascribed to SIMONE DA PESARO.

65. VIRGIN AND CHILD.

Half-length figure of the Virgin, seated, to left ; gold dress, black hood, and mantle ; the Infant Christ on her knee ; they hold a necklace of coral beads ; behind two angels. Panel 26 × 18½ in.

By MATTEO DA SIENA.   Lent by C. FAIRFAX MURRAY, ESQ.

66. St. Albinus and St. Bernard.

Small half-length figures of the saints, in episcopal dress, wearing mitres, standing to left behind a parapet ; on the right St. Bernard in attitude of devotion, his crozier resting against his shoulder ; on the left St. Albinus, his right hand on his breast, his left resting on open book on parapet.   Panel 13 × 17½ in.

By Masaccio.   Lent by the Earl of Ashburnham.

67.   St. John Gualbert instituting the Order of Vallombrosa.

Small full-length figures : a novice of the Order kneeling to left receiving the habit from St. John Gualbert ; other monks stand around.   Panel 12 × 15½ in.

By Masaccio.   Lent by Henry Wagner, Esq.

68.   Triptych.

In the centre the crucifixion with St. Mary Magdalen at the foot of the cross ; the Virgin swooning among the Holy Women on the left ; the Apostles and Longinus on the right ; spectators in the background ; on the wings on the left are depicted the Nativity with the crucifixion of St. Peter above ; and on the right the Virgin enthroned with saints ; above a scene from the life of St. Nicholas ; inscription below with date 1338; gothic frame.   Panel 24 × 32 in.

By Taddeo Gaddi.   Lent by William Fuller Maitland, Esq.

69.   St. Ubaldus and St. Fridian.

Small half-length figures of the saints in episcopal dress, wearing mitres, standing to right behind a parapet ; on the right St. Fridian holding crozier is addressing St. Ubaldus ; on his right his hands crossed ; on the parapet lie books.   Panel 13 × 17½ in.

By Masaccio.   Lent by the Earl of Ashburnham.

70.   Christ Bearing the Cross.

Small full-length figure of Christ, to right, bearing the Cross ; behind, small figure of Dominican monk kneeling in prayer ; gold background.   Panel 12 × 8½ in.

By Berna da Siena.   Lent by Sir Frederick Leighton, Bart., P.R.A.

71.   Volto Santo di Lucca.

Full-length life size figure of Christ, standing facing, his arms outstretched in a line with the cross behind ; he is clothed in royal dalmatic ; under his feet the chalice ; on the left kneels St. John the Baptist, and behind him St. Vincent Ferrer ; on the right kneels St. Mark, and behind him St. Antoninus ; in the background a mandorla of angels and cherubim.   Panel 72 × 79 in.

Cosimo Roselli.   Lent by William Fuller Maitland, Esq.

72. VIRGIN AND CHILD.

Under life-size, half-length figure of the Virgin seated, facing, beneath a portico, holding the Infant Saviour, Who has in His right hand a carnation, and in His left the orb ; architectural background.   Panel 23½ × 18 in.

By BALDASSARE PERUZZI.   Lent by CHARLES BUTLER, ESQ.

73. VIRGIN AND CHILD.

Half-length figure, under life-size, of the Virgin, facing, head to left, holding the Infant Saviour, His right hand raised in benediction ; left holds bird ; behind are two attendant angels ; gold background, richly ornamented.   Panel 25 × 15½ in.

By BENVENUTO DA SIENA.   Lent by HORACE BUTTERY, ESQ.

74. THE CRUCIFIXION.

In the centre Christ on the Cross ; on the left a group with the Virgin swooning and the Holy Women, and Longinus the centurion kneeling ; on the right St. John and another Saint ; groups of spectators behind.   Panel 11 × 20 in.

By GIOTTINO.   Lent by ISAAC FALCKE, ESQ.

75. TRIPTYCH.

In the centre the Virgin seated facing, holding the Infant Child ; before her are St. Stephen and St. Catherine, and on either side St. Peter and St. Paul ; on the wings are depicted the Scourging, the Crucifixion, and the Annunciation.   Panel 17 × 19 in.

FLORENTINE SCHOOL.   Lent by MRS. HENRY GORDON.

76. TWO APOSTLES.

Half-length figures of St. Mark and St. Thomas facing ; gold background : architectural frame with small portraits and ornaments.   Panel 17½ × 19½ in.   From the Fuller Russell Collection.

This picture belonged to an altar-piece, of which No. 26 formed a part.

By UGOLINO DA SIENA.   Lent by HENRY WAGNER, ESQ.

77. THE STORY OF JOSEPH.

On the left a colonnaded building within which is seen Joseph seated on a throne receiving his brethren, and outside the brethren filling their sacks with corn ; on the right the brethren about to load their camels and to start, and Joseph discovering the cup in Benjamin's sack ; in the background the brethren returning to their own land ; on the extreme right a giraffe.   Panel 17 × 64½ in.   (See also No. 59.)

By PESELLINO.   :   Lent by C. BRINSLEY MARLAY, ESQ.

78. THE SAINTS OF THE DESERT: A "THEBAID."

This picture contains in a variety of groups incidents from the lives of the Saints of the Desert, amongst whom may be noted St. Jerome, St. Benedict, St. Antony, St. Francis d'Assisi, &c. Panel 18¼ × 6¼ in. (See No. 79.)

There are similar pictures in the Campo Santo of Pisa, and in the Uffizi Gallery at Florence.

By AMBROGIO LORENZETTI.   Lent by the EARL OF CRAWFORD, K.T.

79. THE HERMIT SAINTS OF THE DESERT: A "THEBAID."

This picture gives scenes from the lives of the Hermit Saints who lived in Egypt and Syria during the third and fourth centuries. Panel 31 × 89 in. (See No. 78.)

By AMBROGIO LORENZETTI.   Lent by the EARL OF CRAWFORD, K.T.

80. THE CORONATION OF THE VIRGIN.

Christ on the left in the act of placing a crown on the head of the Virgin who is on the right; full-length figure of an angel on each side holding up a crimson curtain, which encloses the whole of the picture; round the two principal figures is a mandorla of cherubim and seraphim. Panel (semi-circular) 34 × 86 in.

By FILIPPO LIPPI.   Lent by the MARQUESS OF LOTHIAN, K.T.

81. THE TRIUMPH OF LOVE.

On a golden car drawn by two richly caparisoned horses ridden by two negroes stands a figure of Love with drawn bow ; also on the car are three cupids ; around are figures in early Florentine costumes ; in front figures with Aristotle and Phyllis, and Samson and Delilah. On the reverse on a ground-work of flowers a crane and two coats-of-arms said to be the arms of the Strozzi family. Panel, octagonal, 24 in.

A companion picture to this is in the Royal Gallery at Turin.

By DELLO DELLI.   Lent by HENRY WAGNER, ESQ.

WEST GALLERY.

SECOND ROOM.

MASTERS OF THE XIV.—XV. CENTURIES.

82. ECCE HOMO.

Head of Christ, slightly under life-size, facing, crowned with thorns ; behind, curtain and fruit ; landscape background. The frame is inscribed FRANCISCUS GENTILIS DE FABRIANO. Panel 16½ × 11½ in.

By GENTILE DA FABRIANO.   Lent by LUDWIG MOND, ESQ.

83. PORTRAIT OF ANGELUS POLITIAN, POET (1454-1494).

Bust portrait of the Poet, to left ; long hair, brown dress, red cap ; background of bay leaves with birds. Panel 15 × 11½ in. Formerly in the Guadagni collection.

Born at Monte Pulciano in Tuscany, took his name from the Latin appellation of his birthplace, "Mons Politianus," his real name being *Benedict de Cinis ;* was employed by Lorenzo de' Medici as preceptor to his children, and by him made Prior of the College of S. Giovanni ; he afterwards received a canonry in the cathedral at Florence.

By LORENZO DI CREDI.   Lent by LORD WINDSOR.

84. HYLAS AND THE NAIADS.

The scene is laid in a flowery meadow ; the Naiads surround the half-drowned boy, some bringing him offerings of flowers, another a little Bologna white dog, another drops her flowers in her excitement, while yet another, bolder than the rest, lays hold of him to raise him from the ground ; rocky background, trees, birds, and flowers. Canvas 61 × 68 in.

Hylas, son of Theiodamas, King of the Dryopes, was a favourite of Heracles, who took him with him when he joined the expedition of the Argonauts. Landing on the coast of Mysia Hylas went to fetch water for Heracles ; but when he came to the well his beauty excited the Naiads, who drew him down into the water and he was never seen again. The inhabitants of Prusa celebrated a festival to Hylas, and on that occasion the people of the neighbourhood roamed over the mountain calling out his name.

By PIETRO DI COSIMO.   Lent by R. H. BENSON, ESQ.

85. THE STORY OF CUPID AND PSYCHE.

A series of scenes from the legend of Cupid and Psyche. Probably the front of a cassone. Panel 23 × 70 in. (See also No. 146). From the Fisch and Brett collections.

By FILIPPO LIPPI.   Lent by C. BRINSLEY MARLAY, ESQ.

86. ST. LAWRENCE AND ST. PHILIP.

Full-length figures of St. Lawrence holding palm and gridiron, and St. Philip holding cross, fishes, and book. Panel 19 × 14 in.

By BERNARDO DI MARIOTTI.   Lent by DR. J. P. RICHTER.

87. PORTRAIT OF ANDREA DEL VERROCCHIO.

Under life-size half-length figure of Verrocchio facing, his hands, crossed, rest on table before him; in right stile; dark dress and cap with two feathers, fastened by a jewel; around neck chain with pendant jewel, a fleur de lis; on the right, small seated antique figure; on the left, window through which is seen landscape; his cap is inscribed in gold letters, LORENZO DI CREDI. Panel 18 × 14½ in.

Sculptor, painter and musician; born at Florence in 1432; a pupil of Donatello; is celebrated for his works in bronze and notably for the "David" in the Uffizi Gallery; died in 1488.

By LORENZO DI CREDI.   Lent by FREDERICK A. WHITE, ESQ.

88. ST. BARBARA.

Small full-length figure of St. Barbara to right, holding a castle and standing on the figure of a king; before her kneels a youth; in background, mountains with sea and fortified city; in the left is represented the martyrdom of the Saint. Panel 27 × 18½ in.

SCHOOL OF POLLAIUOLO.   Lent by the EARL OF CRAWFORD, K.T.

89. PORTRAIT OF A YOUNG MAN.

Half-length figure to the left, looking at the spectator, red dress, black cap; landscape background. Panel 70 × 14½ in.

By FRANCIABIGIO.   Lent by W. VASEL, ESQ.

90. VIRGIN AND CHILD WITH ANGELS.

In the centre full-length figure of the Virgin seated facing, the Child upon her knees; on either side an angel in attitude of adoration; landscape. Panel, circular, 42½ in.

By FRANCESCO GRANACCI.   Lent by WILLIAM FULLER MAITLAND, ESQ.

C

91. THE MARRIAGE FEAST OF PERITHOUS AND HIPPODAMEIA.

In the foreground an open colonnade; beneath it a table, at which are nine guests feasting, attended by Centaurs; two musicians on the left; landscape with rocks and buildings in the background.   Panel 31 × 51 in.   See also No. 97.   From the Barker collection.

On the marriage of Perithous, the leader of the Lapithæ, and Hippodameia, the Centaurs who had long been at war with the Lapithæ but with whom peace had lately been concluded, were invited to the feast.   In the midst of the entertainment the quarrel was revived (see No. 97), which ended in a bloody war in which the Lapithæ were defeated.

By LUCA SIGNORELLI.   Lent by MRS. AUSTEN AND
                          THE TRUSTEES OF THE LATE J. F. AUSTEN, ESQ.

92. VIRGIN AND CHILD.

Three-quarter length figure of the Virgin seated to right, the Infant Saviour on her knees; gold background with arabesques; in the top corners are busts of Julius Cæsar and Domitian.   Panel 32 × 30½ in.

By LUCA SIGNORELLI.

93. VIRGIN AND CHILD.

Three-quarter length figure to left of the Virgin in attitude of adoring the Infant Saviour, who stands on a stone pedestal and is supported by an angel; in the background flowers on either side.   Panel 27½ × 18½ in.

By ANTONIO POLLAIUOLO.   Lent by LORD BATTERSEA.

94. THE ASSUMPTION OF THE VIRGIN.

Above, the Virgin seated in glory between adoring angels; below are the twelve Apostles surrounding the empty tomb, on the edge of which kneels St. Thomas receiving the girdle; at the bottom in the front a small picture of the Crucifixion; below, a predella decorated with eight flying angels.   Panel, measurement with the frame, 112 × 102 in.   From the Dudley collection.

By LORENZO DI BICCI.   Lent by W. E. S. ERLE DRAX, ESQ.

95. VIRGIN AND CHILD.

Three-quarter length figure of the Virgin seated to left, the Child upon her knees, background of pink and white roses.   Panel 23¼ × 15¼ in.

By FILIPPO LIPPI.   Lent by LORD BATTERSEA.

96. VIRGIN AND CHILD.

Three-quarter length figure of the Virgin standing slightly to the left in a chamber before a wall, the Child in her arms with His arms around her neck; landscape seen through a window on left; on the right in a niche a vase of roses; on the wall are an open book and a goldfinch.   Panel 31 × 21½ in.

By SANDRO BOTTICELLI.   Lent by CHARLES BUTLER, ESQ.

97. FIGHT BETWEEN THE CENTAURS AND THE LAPITHÆ.

On the left in the foreground an open colonnade, under it the table upset and the Centaurs attacking a group of women ; on the right a battle between the Centaurs and Lapithæ ; landscape background. Panel 31 × 51 in. This picture is a sequel to No. 91. From the Barker collection.

By LUCA SIGNORELLI.   Lent by MRS. AUSTEN AND
          THE TRUSTEES OF THE LATE J. F. AUSTEN, ESQ.

98. A RIPOSO.

The Virgin kneeling to left in adoration before the Infant Christ, Who lies on the ground ; on the right St. Joseph sleeping ; on the left three angels in adoration holding flowers and book ; landscape background with rocks and sea. Panel, circular, 38 in.

By LORENZO DI CREDI.   Lent by SIR BERNHARD SAMUELSON, BART., M.P.

99. PORTRAIT OF A YOUNG MAN.

Half-length figure to left, fair hair, dark grey cloak, and cap. Panel 22 × 16 in.

By PIETRO POLLAIUOLO.   Lent by The MISSES LOUISA AND LUCY COHEN.

100. VIRGIN AND CHILD.

In a landscape the Virgin kneeling to the left in adoration of the Child Who lies before her. Panel 27 × 18 in. From the Dudley collection.

By GHIRLANDAIO.   Lent by C. BRINSLEY MARLAY, ESQ.

101. VIRGIN AND CHILD WITH ST. CHRISTINA AND ST. CATHERINE OF ALEXANDRIA.

Small full-length figures ; the Virgin seated on a marble throne in the centre, the Child on her knees and two angels holding a crown over her head ; on the left stands St. Christina, and on the right St. Catherine of Alexandria ; in foreground vase with flowers and bust of nun in prayer. Panel 26 × 16 in. From the Barker collection.

By COSIMO ROSELLI.   Lent by C. BRINSLEY MARLAY, ESQ.

102. VIRGIN AND CHILD.

Half-length figure of the Virgin to right, holding the Infant Saviour Who stands on a parapet before her ; gold diapered background. Panel 26 × 15 in.
          Lent by CONSTANTINE A. IONIDES, ESQ.

103. VIRGIN AND CHILD AND ST. JOHN.

Three-quarter length figure of the Virgin, seated, facing, the Infant Christ on her lap, His right hand raised in act of blessing the infant St. John, who stands in adoration

                   C 2

on the left; in His left hand pomegranate; landscape seen through windows in the background. Panel, circular, 29 in.

By SANDRO BOTTICELLI.   Lent by HENRY WILLETT, ESQ.

104. CASSONE.

(1) Marriage Scene. On the back panel is seen on the left the arrival of the bridegroom with his retinue of knights and his reception by the father of the bride and the bride, who are accompanied by attendants and knights; on the right the marriage feast with people dancing before the bride and bridegroom and their attendants; in the background buildings and sea with boats; below are the arms of the Avansati family. (2) War between the Persians and the Greeks. On the front panel Darius, seated on a canopied car, is departing for the war against Alexander the Great; he is followed by his mother and wife who are seated in another car and surrounded by their children on foot; retinue of soldiers and horsemen; in the background landscape with cities. (3) Story of Apollo and Daphne. On the left end panel Apollo pursuing Daphne, and on the right end one Daphne changed into a tree, the trunk of which is embraced by Apollo. Panel (1) 17 × 68½ in., (2) 16 × 56 in. (3) 16 × 14½ in. each.

The portrait of the bride, of whom there is a painting in the inside of the cover of the cassone, is seen in the bride on the back panel and also in the representations of Daphne on the end panels. (See also No. 124).

FLORENTINE SCHOOL.   Lent by the EARL OF CRAWFORD, K.T.

105. PORTRAITS OF FRANCESCO SASSETTI AND HIS SON.

Three-quarter length figure of Francesco Sassetti seated facing, wearing red fur-trimmed tunic and crimson cap; his right hand rests on his chair; his eyes are turned towards his son who stands on his left and looks up to him; the latter wears grey brocaded dress trimmed with white fur, dark green slashed under-sleeves, and scarlet cap; through a window behind is the sea and mountainous landscape with buildings. The window frame is inscribed, FRANCISCUS SAXETTUS THEODORUS. Panel 29½ × 20½ in.

Ghirlandaio executed a fresco of Francesco Sassetti and his wife in the Sassetti Chapel in Sta. Trinita at Florence. From the Graham collection.

By GHIRLANDAIO.   Lent by R. H. BENSON, ESQ.

106. VIRGIN AND CHILD WITH ATTENDANT ANGELS.

Three-quarter figure of the Virgin, half life-size, seated to front in grey drapery; on her lap the Child, with a coral necklace and amulet about His neck; three angels standing behind. Panel 33 × 22½ in.

By PIERO DELLA FRANCESCA.   Lent by CHRIST CHURCH, OXFORD.

107. VIRGIN AND CHILD AND SAINTS.

Small full-length figures ; the Virgin seated, facing ; erect on her knees is the Infant Christ ; two angels behind ; on the left stand St. Anthony and St. Jerome, and on the right St. Louis of Toulouse and St. George and two female Saints. Panel 10 × 9 in.

By PESELLINO.   Lent by CAPT. G. L. HOLFORD, C.I.E.

108. THE HOLY FAMILY AND ST. JOHN THE BAPTIST.

Within a ruin the Virgin kneeling adoring the Infant Saviour, who lies on the ground ; on the left is seated St. Joseph and in the background stands St. John the Baptist in attitude of adoration ; city in the background. Panel, circular, 36 in.

By SANDRO BOTTICELLI.   Lent by WICKHAM FLOWER, ESQ.

109. FLYING ANGEL.

Small full-length figure of an angel in attitude of adoration flying downwards to left. Panel 15½ × 24 in.

By FLORENTINE SCHOOL.   Lent by the COUNTESS BROWNLOW.

110. PORTRAIT OF ESMERALDA BANDINELLI.

Half-length figure of a lady in a room slightly turned to left, facing the spectator ; red dress ; her right raised and resting against the sill of a window. Panel 25 × 15½ in. This portrait represents the same head that appears in the central personage of Botticelli's *Spring* at Florence.

By SANDRO BOTTICELLI.   Lent by CONSTANTINE A. IONIDES, ESQ.

111. VIRGIN AND CHILD.

Three-quarter length figure of the Virgin, standing in a recess, facing, holding the Infant Jesus, Who stands upon a pedestal and holds a pomegranate in His left hand ; in the background bank of pink roses. Panel, circular top, 39 × 25 in.

By SANDRO BOTTICELLI.   Lent by LORD BATTERSEA.

112. THE DEPARTURE OF THE ARGONAUTS.

On the left Jason and the Argonauts, conspicuous amongst whom is Hercules, taking leave of his father Æson before starting on their voyage ; on the right their embarkation and the departure of the ship Argo, with the rocks of the Symplegades in the distance. Panel 32½ × 63½ in. (See also No. 117.)

By FILIPPINO LIPPI.   Lent by the EARL OF ASHBURNHAM.

113. VIRGIN AND CHILD WITH ST. CLARE AND ST. AGATHA.

In the centre, standing before a throne, the Virgin holding the Infant Christ Who has a crown in His left hand ; on the left kneels St. Clare, and on the right, St. Agatha ; behind on either side of the throne are two Angels wearing wreaths of flowers ; sky background. Panel 52×41 in. From the Brett collection.

By FILIPPO LIPPI.   Lent by MRS. AUSTEN AND
                            THE TRUSTEES OF THE LATE J. F. AUSTEN, ESQ.

114. VIRGIN AND CHILD AND ST. JOHN.

The Virgin kneeling to left among ruins in adoration of the Child, Who lies on a cushion beside her ; to left the infant St. John in attitude of adoration ; mountainous landscape with buildings in the background. Panel, circular, 34 in.

By LORENZO DI CREDI.   Lent by S. SCROPE, ESQ.

115. VIRGIN AND CHILD ENTHRONED.

Full-length under life-size figure of the Virgin seated facing in a very richly ornamented shrine ; the Infant Christ is seated on a cushion on her right knee playing with a jewel which hangs from her mantle ; landscape background. Panel 34½ × 25 in.

By BERNARDINO PINTURICCHIO.   Lent by CHARLES BUTLER, ESQ.

116. PORTRAIT OF A LADY.

Half-length life-size profile to left, flowered brocade dress. Panel 20½ × 14 in.
By PIERO DELLA FRANCESCA.   Lent by The EARL OF ASHBURNHAM.

117. THE ARGONAUTS IN COLCHIS.

A number of scenes in the story of the cruise of the Argonauts under Jason in search of the Golden Fleece, representing the arrival of the Argonauts in Colchis, the meeting of Jason and Medea, the banquet given to Jason by Aetes, the field sown with dragons' teeth, and ploughed, and the combatants who arise from the seed, Jason killing the dragon through the spells of Medea, the seizure of the Golden Fleece by Jason and the flight of Medea and Jason to the ship Argo. Panel 32½ × 63½. (See also No. 112.)

By BENOZZO GOZZOLI.   Lent by The EARL OF ASHBURNHAM.

118. VIRGIN AND CHILD WITH ANGELS.

Small full-length figure of the Virgin, standing facing between two angels before a balcony, holding the Infant Saviour, Who sleeps on her left arm, and in her right hand a book on which His foot rests ; the angels are playing lyre and pipes ; landscape background. Panel, circular, 33 in.

By RAFFAELLINO DEL GARBO.   Lent by SIR BERNHARD SAMUELSON, Bart., M.P.

119. THE BAPTISM OF ST. APOLLONIA.

In the desert St. Apollonia kneeling ; to left an angel baptising her: on the right St. Leoninus.   Panel 15 × 23 in.

By FRANCESCO GRANACCI.   Lent by C. FAIRFAX MURRAY, ESQ.

120. ST. NICHOLAS.

Small half-length figure in circular medallion of St. Nicholas in bishop's robes, holding book and crozier.   Panel 6 × 6 in.

By FRA ANGELICO.   Lent by LADY LINDSAY.

121. VIRGIN AND CHILD.

Within a room, three-quarter length figure of the Virgin, facing, holding the Infant Child, Who stands on the corner of a parapet, with pomegranate in His left hand and red berries in His right ; through the window is seen a landscape. Panel 25 × 21 in.

By SANDRO BOTTICELLI.   Lent by LADY LINDSAY.

122. VIRGIN AND CHILD AND ST. JOHN.

Under an arch, half-length life-size figure of the Virgin, seated to left, holding the Infant Christ erect on her knees ; He places His arms around her neck ; on the left the infant St. John in adoration, resting his elbow on vase of flowers ; landscape back-ground.   Panel 33½ × 26 in.

By GHIRLANDAIO.   Lent by MRS. AUSTEN AND
                                          THE TRUSTEES OF THE LATE J. F. AUSTEN, ESQ.

123. VIRGIN AND CHILD WITH ST. JOHN.

Before a rock the Virgin kneeling to left, in adoration over the Infant Christ, Who lies on the ground before her ; on her right the infant St. John holding scroll and cross ; landscape background with buildings.   Panel, circular, 34 in.

BY SANDRO BOTTICELLI.   Lent by WILLIAM FULLER MAITLAND, ESQ.

124. CASSONE.

(1) Marriage festivities, &c.   On the back panel, within a city on the right is seen an assembly of men and women witnessing the feats of acrobats ; in the centre other men pursuing women ; on the left outside the walls of the city a combat of knights, all in Florentine costume ; below, the arms of the Reddici family. (2) Battle of Issus.   In the front panel is depicted the battle of Issus between the troops of

Darius, who is seated on a canopied car and those of Alexander the Great, who is seen on horseback amongst the belligerents; on the left Alexander receiving the mother, wife and children of Darius. (3) Story of Apollo and Phaeton. On the left-end panel Phaeton kneeling before Apollo, and demanding of him to drive his chariot, and on the right-end one the fall of Phaeton. Panel: (1) 17¼ × 68¼ in; (2) 16 × 56 in ; (3) 16 × 14½ in. each.

The portrait of the bridegroom of whom there is a painting on the inside of the cover is seen in the seated figure on the right of the back panel, and also in that of Apollo on the left-end panel. (See also No. 104.)

FLORENTINE SCHOOL.   Lent by the EARL OF CRAWFORD, K.T.

125. VIRGIN AND CHILD WITH ST. FRANCIS AND ST. ELIZABETH.

Figures slightly under life-size ; in the centre half-length figure of the Virgin, facing, holding the Infant Christ on a cushion on a parapet, Who touches a book which the Virgin holds in her right hand ; on the right St. Francis ; on the left St. Elizabeth ; in the background is depicted the Flight into Egypt; the parapet is decorated with bas-reliefs of the giving of the Law, Moses throwing down the tables of stone before the golden calf, and the destruction of idols. Panel 33½ × 27½ in.

By GHIRLANDAIO.   Lent by the EARL OF LEICESTER.

126. VIRGIN AND CHILD WITH ANGELS.

Small three-quarter length figure of the Virgin, seated to left, with the Child standing on her lap, holding her dress with both His hands ; in her left hand is a golden ball ; two angels stand by on the left, holding a scroll and singing ; landscape background. Panel 19 × 14 in.

By PINTURICCHIO.   Lent by Lieut.-Col. W. CORNWALLIS WEST.

127. ST. AUGUSTINE.

Full-length life-size figure of St. Augustine, standing to right, wearing gold brocade cope and jewelled mitre ; his left hand, wearing glove and rings, holds crozier ; his right, also gloved and jewelled, re.ts on shoulder of the donor, who kneels to right in attitude of prayer with his cap on his hands. Panel 54¾ × 25 in.

From the Litta and Prince Napoleon's collections ; formerly in the Certosa of Pavia.

By AMBROGIO BORGOGNONE.   Lent by HENRY HUCKS GIBBS, ESQ.

128. THE TRIUMPH OF JEPHTHAH.

Scene representing Jephthah riding on horseback to the left, towards the walls of a city ; behind, a group of horsemen holding branches, before him another group of foot soldiers, one of them a negro ; on the left a procession of women headed by Jephthah's daughter is issuing from the city to meet him. Panel 13½ × 32 in. Probably the front of a cassone.

FLORENTINE SCHOOL   Lent by the EARL OF CRAWFORD, K.T.

129. THE TRIUMPH OF FAME, TIME, AND RELIGION.

On the left a group representing the triumph of Fame, with figure of Fame on a car drawn by two white horses, two captives before it ; in the centre, towards the right, figure of Time, seated on a car drawn by two stags ; on the right, figure of Christ attended by angels, seated in glory above the firmament, on which are the emblems of St. Mark and St. John, and below which is seen the earth surrounded by the ocean.   Panel 16½ × 61 in. (See also No. 139.)

Probably the front of a cassone.

By PIERO DI COSIMO.   Lent by MRS. AUSTEN AND
                   THE TRUSTEES OF THE LATE J. F. AUSTEN, ESQ.

130. THE NATIVITY.

In a stable, life-size figure of the Virgin kneeling to left in adoration over the Infant Christ, Who lies on her robe ; on the left, St. Joseph seated, asleep, holding a staff ; in the background are seen the three kings approaching on horseback with a troop of attendants.   Panel, circular, 48½ in.

By SANDRO BOTTICELLI.   Lent by MRS. AUSTEN AND
                   THE TRUSTEES OF THE LATE J. F. AUSTEN, ESQ.

131. VIRGIN AND CHILD WITH SAINTS.

Small full-length figure of the Virgin, seated facing, holding the Infant Saviour ; on the left kneels St. Nicholas of Bari, and on the right St. Antony of Padua ; above on either side an angel in adoration.   Panel 17 × 11½ in.

SCHOOL OF SIGNORELLI.   Lent by ISAAC FALCKE, ESQ.

132. PORTRAIT OF ANTONELLO DA MESSINA, PAINTER.

Small bust portrait of the Painter, to left, in black dress and cap.   Panel 10¼ × 7½ in.

Born at Messina *circ.* 1421, studied in Flanders, and afterwards played an important part in the introduction of oil painting into Italy ; he worked chiefly at Messina, Milan, Venice, where it is believed that he died, *circ.* 1493.

By HIMSELF.   Lent by HENRY WILLETT, ESQ.

133. VIRGIN AND CHILD.

Small half-length figure of the Virgin, standing before a balustrade, on which is the Infant Christ erect ; His left arm around her neck ; on the right in the distance is a town on a rock.   Panel 13 × 11 in.

By ANDREA SOLARIO.   Lent by the EARL OF NORTHBROOK.

134. VIRGIN AND CHILD AND ST. JOHN.

Three-quarter life-size figure of the Virgin seated to left, holding in her arms the Infant Saviour, Who embraces her ; before her, table with book and cushion, behind

which stands St. John the Baptist, his hands clasped and bearing cross.   Panel
36 × 25 in.   From the Marq. de Bammeville and Leyland collections
By SANDRO BOTTICELLI.   Lent by MESSRS. D. and P. COLNAGHI.

135. VIRGIN AND CHILD AND ST. JOHN.

Within a building the Virgin kneeling to left in adoration of the Child, Who lies on a
cushion before her ; the infant St. John in adoration behind ; through the arches of
the building is seen a landscape.   Panel, circular, 28½ in.
By LORENZO DI'CREDI.   Lent by W. E. S. ERLE DRAX, ESQ.

136. THE MARTYRDOM OF ST. CECILIA.

The Saint standing in a cauldron over a fire ; above her are angels ; on the left on a
throne is seated a Roman governor ; in front soldiers.   Panel 17½ × 11 in.
SCHOOL OF SIGNORELLI.   Lent by ISAAC FALCKE, ESQ.

137. PORTRAIT OF A MAN.

Bust portrait to left in black dress and cap ; to left, landscape.   Panel 12 × 10 in.
By ANTONELLO DA MESSINA.   Lent by the MISSES LOUISA AND LUCY COHEN.

138. VIRGIN AND CHILD WITH SAINTS AND DONORS.

Small full-length figure of the Virgin, seated facing on a throne, the Infant Saviour
on her knees, between St. Dominic and St. Catherine of Siena ; in front kneel two
Donors ; landscape background.   Panel 14 × 12¼ in.   From the Dudley collection.
By ANDREA D'ASSISI.   Lent by WICKHAM FLOWER, ESQ.

139. THE TRIUMPH OF LOVE, CHASTITY, AND DEATH.

On the left a group of Florentine nobles surrounding car drawn by four white horses
on which stands figure of Cupid with drawn bow ; in the centre, towards the right, a
group of women surrounding car drawn by two unicorns in which is seated a figure
of Chastity, with the figure of Love in bondage ; in the extreme right, car drawn by
two black oxen, with figure of Death.   Panel 16½ × 61 in.   (See also No. 129.)
Probably the front of a cassone.
By FIERO DI COSIMO.   Lent by MRS. AUSTEN AND
                                    THE TRUSTEES OF THE LATE J. F. AUSTEN, ESQ.

140. VIRGIN AND CHILD AND ST. JOHN.

Three-quarter length figure of the Virgin seated to left, holding on her knees the
Infant Saviour ; her right hand touches the cheek of the infant St. John who kneels
in adoration ; on the left an angel presenting a pomegranate to Christ, and on the right
another angel ; in the background landscape.   Panel, circular, 44 in.
By RAFFAELLINO DEL GARBO.

141. VIRGIN AND CHILD WITH ANGELS.

Full-length figure of the Virgin seated facing, holding on her knees the Holy Child, Who has a book in His right hand; on each side are two angels playing musical instruments; the Virgin and Child have halos and ornaments in gesso with jewels inserted. Panel 50½ × 25 in.

By BUTTINONE.   Lent by COLONEL JEKYLL, R.E.

142. THE JUDGMENT OF PARIS.

On the right Paris, seated to left, with the goddesses standing before him, is giving the apple, inscribed TH ΚΑΛH, to Venus; at his feet lies a dog and behind are a goat and cattle; on the left the three goddesses are again seen, Venus holding the apple in her right hand and showing it to Jupiter; the two groups are divided by a tree; hilly landscape with water in the background. Panel 23 × 41 in.

FLORENTINE SCHOOL.   Lent by CHARLES BUTLER, ESQ.

143. THE BIRTH OF ST. JOHN THE BAPTIST.

In a chamber on the left a group of four women and one man; one of the women is seated on the ground holding the Infant St. John above a basin, into which another is pouring water from a jug; on the right St. Elizabeth in a bed, at the foot of which is seated Zacharias writing on paper. Panel 9½ × 17 in.

By LUCA SIGNORELLI.   Lent by the EARL OF CRAWFORD, K.T.

144. VIRGIN AND CHILD.

Small three-quarter-length figure of the Virgin seated, facing; the Infant Christ upon her lap; landscape background. Panel 13½ × 9½ in.

By LORENZO DI CREDI.   Lent by LORD BALCARRES.

145. THE STORY OF ST. JOACHIM.

In a landscape on the left the Angel appearing in a vision to St. Joachim; on the right the meeting of St. Joachim and St. Anne at the Golden Gate; in the background the expulsion of St. Joachim from the Temple. Panel 9½ × 17 in.

By LUCA SIGNORELLI.   Lent by the EARL OF CRAWFORD, K.T.

146. THE STORY OF CUPID AND PSYCHE.

A series of scenes for the legend of Cupid and Psyche. Probably the front of a cassone. Panel 16½ × 58½ in. (See also No. 85.)

By FILIPPINO LIPPI.   Lent by CHARLES BUTLER, ESQ.

147. THE STORY OF NASTAGIO DEGLI ONESTI FROM BOCCACCIO'S DECAMERON.

Within a decorated enclosure with trees is spread a table for a feast, the guests mostly standing in attitudes of surprise; in front, in the centre, is seen the figure of a lady running to left, and bitten by dogs, and pursued by a horseman; on the left is seen Nastagio, his arms extended; on the right, wooded background. Panel 27½ × 54 in.

The subject of the story is given under No. 156. The picture, however, belongs to another series.

By SANDRO BOTTICELLI.   Lent by the EARL OF ASHBURNHAM.

148. THE STORY OF CAMILLA.

This scene probably represents an incident in the story of Camilla, daughter of Metabus, *Virg. Æn.* xi., 539 *et seq.* Metabus is seen escaping from Privernum with his daughter, Camilla, in his arms, pursued by the Volscians; he reaches the banks of the Amasenus, which is too swollen to allow of his crossing in safety carrying the child; so invoking the protection of the friendly Diana, who appears in the sky, he binds the babe to his spear and launches her on it across the stream, and, swimming over himself, appears on the right carrying her off in safety. Panel 15×42 in. (See also No. 162.)

Probably the front of a cassone.

By MATTEO DA SIENA.   Lent by CHARLES BUTLER, ESQ.

149. ST. GEORGE.

In a landscape St. George on horseback in armour riding to right, and in the act of striking the dragon in front of him; on the left Princess Cleodolinda flying; in the foreground three corpses; on the right, in the background, three horsemen. Panel 30 × 21½ in.

By LUCA SIGNORELLI.   Lent by SIR WILLIAM FARRER.

150. THE BIRTH OF ST. JOHN THE BAPTIST.

On the left a temple with the angel appearing to Zacharias; in the centre and on the right a building with a colonnade, on the outside of which is seen the Visitation of St. Elizabeth to the Virgin, within the birth of St. John, and on the right Zacharias seated at the fireside. Panel 30 × 59 in.

By GHIRLANDAIO.   Lent by the EARL OF ASHBURNHAM.

151. VISIT OF THE QUEEN OF SHEBA TO SOLOMON.

Procession of numerous figures; in the centre the Queen of Sheba seated on a richly gilt car under a canopy, accompanied by horsemen and attendants all in early

Florentine costumes ; landscape, background showing earlier stages of the journey. Panel 16 × 55 in. (See also No. 161.)

Probably the front of a cassone.

FLORENTINE SCHOOL about 1485.　　　Lent by the EARL OF CRAWFORD, K.T.

152. SPRING.

Small full-length figure of a woman in a garden of roses, carrying a bundle of the flowers in her lap. Panel 31 × 9½ in.

By SANDRO BOTTICELLI.　　　Lent by the EARL OF ROSEBERY, K.G.

153. SUMMER.

Small full-length figure of a woman carrying a sheaf of corn on her head, and another sheaf and a reaping hook in her left hand. Panel 31 × 9½ in.

By SANDRO BOTTICELLI.　　　Lent by the EARL OF ROSEBERY, K.G.

154. DIANA AND ACTÆON.

Diana and her nymphs are standing in a marble bath ; on the right is Actæon approaching with his dogs ; on the left he is turned into a stag and they are devouring him ; mountainous background. Panel (12 sided) 23 in. diameter.

FLORENTINE SCHOOL.　　　Lent by SIR EDWARD BURNE JONES, BART.

155. THE ANNUNCIATION.

The Virgin seated on the right under a colonnade ; the Angel Gabriel entering on the left ; in a landscape background on the left is seen St. Raphael leading Tobias. Panel, circular, 23½ in.

By SANDRO BOTTICELLI.　　　Lent by SIR EDWARD BURNE JONES, BART.

156. THE STORY OF NASTAGIO DEGLI ONESTI.

One scene from the story of Nastagio degli Onesti in Boccaccio's *Decameron.* Two tables standing in an open colonnade, with guests feasting ; men on the right, women on the left ; on each side youths attending. Panel 32 × 55 in.

Nastagio degli Onesti being in love with a daughter of Paolo Traversaro has his suit rejected, the family of the lady being nobler than his own. He accordingly leaves Ravenna for Chiassi ; and one day, while walking disconsolately in the pine woods, sees the apparition of a naked lady pursued by a horseman and dogs. He endeavours ineffectually to defend her ; but the horseman dismounts, and, plunging his sword into her body, tears out her heart and throws it to his dogs, who devour it. He then tells Nastagio that she has to suffer this punishment on the same spot every Friday for her cruelty to him when alive. Nastagio, thinking it would be a warning to his own mistress, invites her to a feast in the woods on the following Friday, and the same apparition then appears, to the great terror of the guests. (See No 147). His mistress relents, and consents to marry him ; and the wedding feast is afterwards held at Ravenna in the palace of the Traversari. This last scene is depicted in the above picture, which is one of a series of four pictures formerly in the Leyland Collection, illustrating other incidents of this story.

By SANDRO BOTTICELLI.   Lent by G. DONALDSON, ESQ.

157. AUTUMN.

Small full-length figure of a woman and a boy crossing a plank over a stream ; she carries a basket full of grapes on her head and another basket shaped like a cornucopia, also full of grapes, on her arm.   Panel 31×9½ in.

By SANDRO BOTTICELLI.   Lent by the EARL OF ROSEBERY, K.G.

158. WINTER.

Small full-length figure of a woman, with a bundle of roots under her arm, warming herself over a fire.   Panel 31 × 9½ in.

By SANDRO BOTTICELLI.   .   Lent by the EARL OF ROSEBERY, K.G.

159. PORTRAIT OF A LADY.

Half-length life-size to left, light brown hair, crimson dress with damasked sleeves and white bodice, white cap which is fastened by a cord with jewel on the forehead, pearl necklace with pendant.   Panel 17¼×13½ in.

By GHIRLANDAIO.   Lent by the EARL OF CRAWFORD, K.T.

160. THE DEATH OF LUCRETIA.

In the centre before a triumphal arch ornamented with bas reliefs Lucretia lies dead upon a bier with the dagger in her bosom ; behind her stands Brutus with drawn sword and around her his comrades in attitudes of sorrow and anger ; on the left within a chamber over which is a bas relief of Judith and Holofernes, is seen Tarquin forcing Lucretia ; and on the right within another chamber, over which is the story of Horatius Cocles, Brutus and his friends finding Lucretia dead.   Panel 21 × 70 in.

By SANDRO BOTTICELLI.   Lent by the EARL OF ASHBURNHAM.

161. SOLOMON RECEIVING THE QUEEN OF SHEBA.

On the right is a scene within the Temple, Solomon receiving the Queen who advances to meet him, having dismounted from her chariot which is seen on the left of the picture.   Panel 16 × 55 in.   A companion picture to No. 151.

FLORENTINE SCHOOL about 1485.   Lent by the EARL OF CRAWFORD, K.T.

162. THE STORY OF CAMILLA.

This scene represents another incident in the story of Camilla (see No. 148), *Virg. Æn.* xi., 648. Camilla and her companions are here seen engaged in the fight between the Latin and the Trojan horse under the walls of Laurentum, which ended in the defeat of the former and the death of Camilla. Panel 15 × 41 in.
Probably the front of a cassone.

By MATTEO DA SIENA.   Lent by CHARLES BUTLER, ESQ.

163. THE VISION OF ST. HUBERT.

In a rocky landscape on the left St. Hubert on horseback surrounded by dogs, before him on the right stands a stag bearing a crucifix between its horns ; other stags, birds and other animals in the background. Panel 21 × 25½ in.

Lent by the EARL OF ASHBURNHAM.

By VITTORE PISANO, HITHERTO ASCRIBED TO ALBERT DÜRER.

164. PORTRAIT OF A LADY (ON A PEDESTAL).

Bust in profile to right ; pink dress, with white lace trimming, and light brown curling hair and light brown cloak, pearl necklace and ornaments in the hair ; window in the background. On the reverse is an Angel standing on the world holding in her left hand an armillary sphere ; trees in the background. Panel 23½ × 16. in.

By SANDRO BOTTICELLI.   Lent by the MISSES LOUISA AND LUCY COHEN.

NORTH GALLERY.

THIRD ROOM.

MASTERS OF THE XV.—XVI. CENTURIES.

165. St. Peter and St. John Healing the Lame Man at the Beautiful Gate of the Temple.

> In the centre stands St. Peter, who with his right hand is raising the lame man lying on the ground ; near him stands St. John in attitude of devotion ; on the left is seen the Beautiful Gate of the Temple ; and on the right spectators and buildings. Panel 12 × 20 in.

By Filippo Lippi.   Lent by W. Fuller-Maitland, Esq.

166. St. George.

> Half-length figure of the saint to right looking up to left ; red cloak and richly embroidered tunic ; holding a palm branch in his left hand ; a nimbus round his head ; sky background.   Panel 24½ × 19 in.

By Ghirlandaio.   Lent by the Marquess of Lothian, K.T.

166*. Three Saints.

> Small half-length figures of St. Blaise in the centre, St. Roch on the left, and St. Julian on the left.   Panel 9½ × 18½ in.

By Girolamo Genga.   Lent by The Misses Louisa and Lucy Cohen.

167. Pieta.

> The Dead Christ between two angels.   Panel 18 × 13 in.

By Giovanni di Bazzi.   Lent by Dr. J. P. Richter.

168. Virgin and Child.

> Small half-length figure of the Virgin facing, the Infant Christ in her arms.   Panel 14 × 11½ in.
>
> From the collection of Count Ghilberto Borromeo.

By Gianpetrino.   Lent by Mrs. Murray, of Newstead.

169. PORTRAIT OF A MAN.

Half-length life-size figure, towards left, looking at the spectator, brown beard, black gown and cap; he holds gloves in his hands.   Panel 29 × 22½ in.

By GIROLAMO ROMANINO.   Lent by the MISSES LOUISA AND LUCY COHEN.

170. CHRIST TEACHING.

Half-length life-size figure of Christ facing; the first finger of the right hand touching the second finger of the left; pink dress with jewelled collar, crossed stole over His shoulders.   Panel 31 × 22½ in.

By BERNARDINO LUINI.   Lent by the MISSES LOUISA and LUCY COHEN.

171. THE LAST SUPPER.

In a large room, Christ seated at a table with the twelve Apostles.   A copy of the large well-known fresco by Leonardo da Vinci at Milan.   Through the windows in the background are seen on the left the Sacrifice of Isaac; on the right the Agony in the Garden.   Panel 27 × 57½ in.

After LIONARDO DA VINCI.   Lent by ROBERT FOX, ESQ.

172. VIRGIN AND CHILD AND ST. JOHN.

Half-length figure of the Virgin before a parapet holding the Infant Christ, Who sits on a cushion His right hand raised in benediction; behind on the left is the infant St. John; landscape background.   Panel 23½ × 19 in.

By GIACOMO FRANCIA.   Lent by CHARLES BUTLER, ESQ.

173. BAPTISM OF ST. AUGUSTINE.

In the centre, within a church, is seen St. Augustine, standing unclothed, and receiving the water of baptism from St. Ambrose; behind St. Ambrose are two acolytes; on the right are St. Monica, mother of St. Augustine, with saints and attendants; and on the left spectators.   Panel 11½ × 18 in.

By PINTURICCHIO   Lent by SIR WILLIAM FARRER.

174. THE RESURRECTION.

In a landscape, Christ standing on the open tomb, banner in His left hand; around four soldiers, three asleep, one in attitude of surprise.   Panel 10½ × 17½ in.   From the Dudley collection.

By PERUGINO.   Lent by F. A. WHITE, ESQ.

D

175. THE VIRGIN AND CHILD AND ST. JOHN.

Full-length figure of the Virgin seated to right, holding the Infant Christ on her knees ; He raises His right hand in benediction of the infant St. John, who kneels facing, looking up at Him and holds his cross ; the Virgin's left hand is placed on His shoulder ; landscape in background seen through a window.   Panel 29½ × 22 in.

By MARCO D'OGGIONNO.

176. VIRGIN AND CHILD.

Half-length figure of the Virgin turned from the spectator, head looking over the left shoulder, the Infant Christ in her arms ; landscape on the left. Panel 19 × 15 in. From the collection of the Contessa Adelaide Garimberti.

By GIANPETRINO.   Lent by MRS. MURRAY, of Newstead.

177. ST. AUGUSTINE PREACHING.

In the centre, within a church, stands St. Augustine preaching ; around him are monks and men and women listening to his discourse.   Panel 11½ × 18 in.

By PINTURICCHIO.   Lent by SIR WILLIAM FARRER.

178. VIRGIN AND CHILD.

Half-length figure of the Virgin to left, holding the Infant Christ, Who stands on a parapet ; they hold together in their right hands a flower.   Panel 28 × 19 in.

By BERNARDINO LUINI.   Lent by the DUKE OF WELLINGTON.

179. ST. MARY MAGDALEN.

Half-length life-size figure of St. Mary Magdalen, to left, head facing, holding cup of ointment.   Panel 26 × 20¾ in.   From the Northwick collection.

By BERNARDINO LUINI.   Lent by W. E. S. ERLE DRAX, ESQ.

180. ST. JOHN THE BAPTIST.

Small full-length figure of St. John seated to left on a rock, drinking from a shell ; in his left hand he holds his cross ; before him, spring pouring from a rock ; landscape background.   Panel 25 × 18½ in.

By GIULIANO BUGIARDINI.   Lent by the EARL OF NORTHBROOK.

181. VIRGIN AND CHILD AND ST. JOHN THE BAPTIST.

Small half-length figure of the Virgin holding the Infant Christ ; in her right hand a garland of flowers; on the right the Infant St. John.   Panel 7½ × 8½ in.   From the collection of the Marquis de San Vitali.

By CORREGGIO (or School of).   Lent by JAMES KNOWLES, ESQ.

182. PORTRAIT OF DON GARCIA DE' MEDICI.

Half-length figure slightly turned to left, in buff slashed dress with red and gold trimming ; short brown hair ; green curtain behind.   Panel 9¼ × 7 in.   Formerly in the Magniac collection.

By ANGELO BRONZINO.   Lent by J. LUMSDEN PROPERT, ESQ., M.D.

183. ST. ANNE ? .

Small full-length figure of the Saint facing, looking to right ; holding a book in her left hand, her right hand raised.   Panel 25 × 13½ in.

Decoration for an altar, executed by order of the Torriani de Mendrisio family.   From the collection of Count Passalacqua of Milan.

By BERNARDINO LUINI.   Lent by J. RUSTON, ESQ.

184. ST. STEPHEN.

Small full-length figure of the Saint standing facing, head to right, in red and green deacon's dress, holding palm in right hand and book in left.   Panel 25 × 13½ in. From the collection of Count Passalacqua of Milan.

By BERNARDINO LUINI.   Lent by J. RUSTON, ESQ.

185. PORTRAIT OF A YOUNG MAN.

Under life-size bust portrait facing, looking to the left, long fair hair, black cap, dark coat trimmed with leopard's skin ; right hand resting on a sill and holding small scroll inscribed with monogram, AMBPR and date 1494.   Panel 21½ × 15 in.

By AMBROGIO DE PREDIS.   Lent by WILLIAM FULLER-MAITLAND, ESQ.

186. VIRGIN AND CHILD.

Half length figure of the Virgin, turned away from the spectator, and looking over her left shoulder, red dress ; she holds the Infant Saviour in her arms.   Panel 20¼ × 14½ in.

By GIANPETRINO.   Lent by HENRY WILLETT, ESQ.

187. ST. JOHN THE BAPTIST.

Half-length figure of the Saint, facing, his right arm turned to right is pointing upwards ; over left shoulder leopard's skin.   Panel 28 × 20½ in.

By LIONARDO DA VINCI.   Lent by H. BENDELACK HEWETSON, ESQ.

188. THE HISTORY OF THREE MARTYRS ON THREE PICTURES.

No. 1.—The three friends setting forth as pilgrims ; in the background they are seen crossing a river in a ferry-boat ; distant view of the gates of a city.   Panel 12½ × 18 in.

No. 2.—This picture is divided into three compartments.   The compartment on the left represents the friends receiving their ordination one as deacon the other two as acolytes ; in the centre they are refusing to sacrifice to Saturn ; in the right the two monks are being stabbed by soldiers.   Panel 12½ × 38½ in.

No. 3.—The last scene represents the three wounded bodies being dragged with ropes by soldiers ; the two acolytes dead, the deacon still praying.   Panel 12½ × 18 in.   From the Passalacqua collection.

By BERNARDINO LUINI.   Lent by E. B.

189. STUDY OF A HEAD.

Small head, to left, of a woman, looking downwards ; in bistre.   Panel 9½ × 6½ in.

By LIONARDO DA VINCI.   Lent by CAPT. G. L. HOLFORD, C.I.E.

190. ST. PETER.

Small full-length figure of St. Peter to right holding book and keys ; above, a small representation of Christ giving the keys to St. Peter ; below, another small representation of the martyrdom of the Saint.   In grisaille.   Panel 9 × 3 in.

By PARMIGIANO.   Lent by the DUKE OF WESTMINSTER, K.G.

191. ST. PAUL.

Small full-length figure of St. Paul to left, holding a book and a sword ; above, a small representation of the conversion of St. Paul, and below, another of his martyrdom, In grisaille.   Panel 9 × 3 in.

By PARMIGIANO.   Lent by the DUKE OF WESTMINSTER, K.G.

192. THREE ANGELS.

Small full-length figures, facing, f three child-angels standing on clouds, looking downwards in attitudes of adoration.   Panel 23 × 29½ in.   This is probably the lunette of a larger picture.

By BERNARDINO LUINI.   Lent by SIR WILLIAM FARRER.

193. St. John the Baptist.

Half-length figure of the Saint facing, his right arm pointing upwards ; over shoulder leopard's skin. Panel 28 × 19½ in.

By Lionardo da Vinci. Lent by W. G. Waters, Esq.

194. Virgin and Child.

Small three-quarter length figure of the Virgin seated facing and looking at the Infant Saviour on her left knee ; her right hand is raised ; the Infant Saviour looks up at the cross which He holds in His left hand ; landscape background. Panel 19 × 14 in.

By Lionardo da Vinci. Lent by Lord Battersea.

195. St. Mary Magdalen.

Half-length figure of St. Mary Magdalen, standing before a porphyry sepulchre, holding a vase in her right hand ; green dress, red mantle. Panel 24½ × 18½ in. Formerly in the Aldobrandini collection at Rome.

By Andrea Solario. Lent by Wickham Flower, Esq.

196. St. George.

Small full-length figure of the Saint, standing, facing, in green dress and red cloak ; banner with red cross in right hand, and palm in left. Panel 25 × 13½ in.

Decoration for an altar executed by order of the Torriani de Mendrisio family. From the collection of Count Passalacqua of Milan.

By Bernardino Luini. Lent by J. Ruston, Esq.

197. St. Catherine of Alexandria.

Small full-length figure of the Saint, facing, looking to left, in green dress and red cloak, palm branch and book in right hand, her left resting on wheel. Panel 25 × 13½ in.

Decoration for an altar, executed by order of the Torriani di Mendrisio family. From the collection of Count Passalacqua of Milan.

By Bernardino Luini. Lent by J. Ruston, Esq.

198. Virgin and Child.

Small figure of the Virgin holding the Infant Jesus in her arms, Whom she is kissing. Panel, oval, 6 × 4½ in.

By Correggio. Lent by the Earl of Carlisle.

199. PORTRAIT OF A MAN.

Bust, life-size, to left, looking at the spectator, black coat and cap.   Panel 17½ × 15½ in.

FLORENTINE SCHOOL.   Lent by HENRY WAGNER, ESQ.

200. VIRGIN AND CHILD.

Three-quarter length figure of the Virgin seated facing, suckling the Infant Christ, Who kneels on her right knee ; red dress and green mantle lined with red.   Panel 25 × 18½ in.

By ANDREA SOLARIO.   Lent by the REV. W. H. WAYNE.

201. ST. JEROME.

Full-length life-size figure of the Saint kneeling, to right, in a landscape, bending over a crucifix, which he holds in his left hand ; on the ground is a book resting on a skull, and beside him his cardinal's hat ; behind him is the lion ; rocky and wooded height in the background, with buildings and the sea in the right distance ; waterfall on the left.   Panel 55 × 44 in.

By GIOVANNI DI BAZZI.   Lent by LUDWIG MOND, ESQ.

202. PORTRAIT OF A LADY.

Half-length life-size figure facing, grey dress, white embroidered chemisette and white coif ; in right hand a pet animal of the marten tribe, the left touching necklet, to which is suspended a jewelled cross.   Panel 29 × 21½ in.

By BERNARDINO LUINI.

203. THE VIRGIN IN ADORATION.

The Virgin kneeling in adoration over the Infant Saviour, Who lies on the ground before her, his head supported on two cushions ; on either side of the Virgin an angel playing musical instrument ; landscape background.   Panel 43 × 27 in.

By ANDREA SOLARIO.   Lent by Dr. J. P. RICHTER.

204. PORTRAIT OF A MAN WITH THE ATTRIBUTES OF DAVID, KING AND PROPHET.

Three-quarter length life-size towards right, wearing crown and furred robe ; his hands folded ; to right, table on which lie papers, inkstand and harp.   Panel 49 × 37½ in. From the Duca Visconti Litta collection.

By LIONARDO DA VINCI.   Lent by HENRY DOETSCH, ESQ.

205. PORTRAIT OF A MAN.

Life-size bust to left, brown beard, black cloak and embroidered doublet, deep white collar. Panel 21½ × 16½ in.

By ANGELO BRONZINO.   Lent by the EARL OF ROSEBERY, K.G.

206. VIRGIN AND CHILD.

Three-quarter length figure of the Virgin facing; the Child in her arms. Panel 24 × 18½ in.

By CESARE DA SESTO.   Lent by HENRY WILLETT, ESQ.

207. THE MARRIAGE OF ST. CATHERINE.

Half-length life-size figure of the Virgin facing, holding with her left arm the Infant Saviour erect on a parapet and about to place a ring on the finger of the right hand of St. Catherine, who kneels on the left, resting her left arm on her wheel ; behind on the right St. Joseph ; landscape background. Panel 25 × 21½ in.

By INNOCENZO DA IMOLA.   Lent by G. DONALDSON, ESQ.

208. VIRGIN AND CHILD.

Small three-quarter length figure of the Virgin seated facing, the Infant Christ on her knees ; she holds His left hand ; red dress, blue mantle ; landscape background. Panel 13½ × 11 in.

By PIETRO PERUGINO.   Lent by HENRY HUCKS GIBBS, ESQ.

209. PORTRAIT OF BARTOLOMEO LIVIANO DI ALVIANO.

Under life-size bust towards right, facing the spectator, brown hair, red dress with green velvet facings, white shirt with black edging, black cap with jewel. Panel 15½ × 12 in.

By JACOPO DE' BARBARI.   Lent by the SOCIETY OF ANTIQUARIES.

210. ANGELS CHANTING.

Two compartments ; six half-length figures of angels, some playing musical instruments, others singing. Panel 13 × 34½ in.

FLORENTINE SCHOOL.   Lent by OWEN DAVIS, ESQ.

211. VIRGIN AND CHILD.

Life-size three-quarter figure of the Virgin, seated facing, head turned to right, holding the Infant Christ, Who is seated on a cushion ; in her left hand an apple. Panel 43 × 32 in.

By PERINO DEL VAGA.   Lent by the EARL OF NORTHBROOK.

212. THE NATIVITY.

The Infant Child lies in a manger in a stable between the Virgin and St. Joseph. On the left stands a shepherd with a lamb in his arms; through a window above is seen an angel appearing to the shepherds.   Panel 69 × 47 in.

By BERNARDINO LUINI.   Lent by E. B.

213. CASSONE.

(1) On the front panel is represented a battle scene of cavalry and foot soldiers of Milan and Florence; on city to the left the banner of the Visconti family; on the city to right the banner of Florence; (2) on the right end panel, knights departing from a castle; (3) on the left end panel knights entering a castle.   Panel (1) 49½ × 17 in.; (2 and 3) 17 × 18 in.

Lent by J. ANNAN BRYCE, ESQ.

214. VIRGIN AND CHILD AND ST. JOHN THE BAPTIST.

Three-quarter length life-size figure of the Virgin seated to left, head facing the spectator, holding on her knees the Infant Christ; whilst the infant St. John stands in adoration by His side.   Panel 41 × 30 in.

By ANDREA DEL SARTO.   Lent by LEOPOLD DE ROTHSCHILD, ESQ.

215. PORTRAIT OF FRANCESCO DE' MEDICI.

Life-size half-length figure seated to left in an armchair, hands resting on a table; left hand holding a miniature portrait; red dress embroidered with gold.   Panel 32 × 25¾ in.

Francesco Maria de' Medici, son of Cosimo, 1st Grand Duke of Tuscany, born 1541; succeeded his father in 1574; created Grand Duke by the Emperor Maximilian in 1576; died 1587.   Married, 1st, Johanna, daughter of the Emperor Ferdinand I.; 2nd, the beautiful Bianca Capello, daughter of a Senator of Venice.

By ANGELO BRONZINO.   Lent by SIR WILLIAM FARRER.

216. THE HOLY FAMILY.

The Virgin kneels in adoration over the Infant Saviour, Who lies before her, supported by three child-angels; two others hover above, holding a scroll; on the left kneels Cardinal Taverna, with his mitre beside him; on the right, near the Virgin, is St. Joseph, with his staff, uncovering his head; stable on the right; distant landscape on the left.   Panel 59 × 45 in.

By GAUDENZIO FERRARI.   Lent by CAPT. G. L. HOLFORD, C.I.E.

217. THE HOLY FAMILY AND ST. JOHN.

Unfinished picture in grisaille ; three-quarter length life-size figure of the Virgin, seated towards the left, holding the Infant Christ upon her lap ; the infant St. John resting against her knees ; in the background on the left St. Joseph. Panel 42 × 32½ in.

By FRA BARTOLOMMEO.   Lent by the EARL OF NORTHBROOK.

218. THE MARTYRDOM OF ST. SEBASTIAN.

In the centre of a landscape stands St. Sebastian tied to a tree ; on the left are two soldiers shooting arrows at the saint, and an old man leaning on his bow ; on the right, Roman general and others; in the background two other soldiers, ruined building, &c. Panel 11 × 30 in.

LOMBARD SCHOOL.   Lent by the EARL OF NORTHBROOK.

219. PORTRAIT OF RAPHAEL.

Small life-size bust of Raphael to left, head facing, wearing black cap and cloak. Panel 14 × 11 in.

By FRANCIABIGIO.   Lent by SIR WILLIAM FARRER.

220. THE HOLY FAMILY.

Small half-length figure of the Virgin to left in adoration over the Infant Saviour, Who is lying on a marble slab, with a pillow under His head ; on the left is St. Joseph ; curtain and sky background.   Panel 17 × 14¼ in.

By GIROLAMO GENGA.   Lent by the REV. W. H. WAYNE.

221. THE INFANT SAVIOUR ADORED BY THE VIRGIN AND SAINTS.

In a mountainous landscape the child lies on a grassy hillock, surrounded by kneeling figures of St. Jerome, St. Catherine of Alexandria, St. Francis, the Virgin and St. Bonaventura ; in the background on the right is seen a cave, the ox and the ass. St. Joseph and a shepherd ; and on the left St. John Baptist preaching, and the arrival of the Magi. Panel 31 × 28 in. Formerly in the Dudley collection.

By VINCENZO CIVERCHIO.   Lent by W. E. S. ERLE DRAX, ESQ.

222. VIRGIN AND CHILD.

Half-length figure of the Virgin facing standing behind a parapet and holding the Infant Christ ; behind, curtain, trees, and landscape, with city in the distance on the left.   Panel 22½ × 17½ in.

By CESARE DA SESTO.   Lent by the MARQUESS OF BUTE, K.T.

223. VIRGIN AND CHILD WITH ST. CATHERINE OF ALEXANDRIA AND ST. CATHERINE OF SIENA.

Small full-length figures ; the Virgin seated facing, on a bank under a tree, the Infant Christ on her knees ; on the right, St. Catherine of Alexandria, on her left St. Catherine of Siena. Panel 15×14 in.

SCHOOL OF CORREGGIO.   Lent by the EARL OF NORTHBROOK.

224. THE HOLY FAMILY AND ST. JOHN THE BAPTIST.

Three-quarter length figure of the Virgin, seated facing, holding on her knees the Infant Jesus, Who is kissing St. John the Baptist ; behind, stands St. Joseph leaning on his staff. Panel 37 × 27 in.

By PERINO DEL VAGA.   Lent by the EARL OF CARLISLE.

225. VIRGIN AND CHILD.

Half-length figure of the Virgin seated facing, holding the Child on her left arm, and with her right hand touching His right, which grasps rose ; on right, behind, curtain ; landscape background. Panel, oval, 27½ × 21 in.

By GIOVANNI DI BAZZI.   Lent by LUDWIG MOND, ESQ.

226. PIETÀ.

Full-length life-size figures ; at the foot of the cross is the Virgin, the dead Christ lying across her knees, Who is supported on the right by St. John, and on the left by St. Mary Magdalen ; behind stand St. Benedict and St. Francis; landscape background. Panel 60 × 58 in. From the Northwick collection.

By TIMOTEO DELLA VITE.   Lent by W. E. S. ERLE DRAX, ESQ.

227. ST. JOHN THE BAPTIST.

Small half-length figure of the Infant Saint to right, head facing ; to right cross with banner. Panel 10¼ × 7½ in.

By ANDREA DEL SARTO.   Lent by the DUKE OF WESTMINSTER, K.G.

228. INFANT ST. JOHN.

Small full-length figure of the Saint holding banner ; landscape background. Panel 9 × 7 in.

By CORREGGIO.   Lent by the EARL OF CARLISLE.

229. THE HOLY FAMILY AND ST. JOHN.

Half-length figure of the Virgin, seated facing, head to right, and looking at the infant St. John around whom she places her left arm, and who raises his hands to the Infant Christ erect on the Virgin's knee and holding cross; the head of St. Joseph appears behind the Infant Christ. Panel 24×18 in.

By FRA BARTOLOMMEO.   Lent by the DUKE OF WESTMINSTER, K.G.

230. THE INFANT SAVIOUR.

Small bust to left, looking at spectator, holding the orb. Panel 10¼ × 7¾ in.

By ANDREA DEL SARTO.   Lent by the DUKE OF WESTMINSTER, K.G.

231. THE MARRIAGE OF ST. CATHERINE.

In a chamber the Virgin seated in profile to the right holding on her knees the Infant Christ, Who is placing the ring on the finger of St. Catherine kneeling with her hand on her wheel; on the left below is the head of St. Joseph and through a door in the background are seen two figures. Panel 9 × 7 in.

By PARMIGIANO.   Lent by the DUKE OF WESTMINSTER, K.G.

232. VIRGIN AND CHILD.

Three-quarter length figure of the Virgin, seated to left, holding the Infant Saviour, His arms round her neck; in her right hand she holds a book; landscape background. Panel 25 × 19 in.

By ANDREA DEL SARTO.   Lent by SIR JAMES LINTON, P.R.I.

233. VIRGIN AND CHILD.

Three-quarter length under life-size figure of the Virgin seated facing, holding the Infant Child on her knees; red dress, green cloak, and green curtain background. Panel 30 × 23 in.

By FRA BARTOLOMMEO.   Lent by Sir WILLIAM FARRER.

234. HEAD OF A SAINT.

Bust facing, black dress with gold edging. Panel 13×10 in.

By PERUGINO.   Lent by LORD BATTERSEA.

235. VIRGIN AND CHILD.

Under life-size half-length figure of the Virgin turned to right, holding the Infant Christ in her arms, Who plays with the veil which falls from her head. Panel 21 × 14½ in.

By GAUDENZIO FERRARI.   Lent by HENRY WILLETT, ESQ.

236. CHRIST IN PRAYER.

Small full-length figures : Christ kneeling in prayer within a chamber into which enter the Holy Women and St. John ; the Virgin raising her right hand. Panel 8 × 8 in.

By CORREGGIO.   Lent by SIR WILLIAM FARRER

237. VIRGIN AND CHILD AND ST. JOHN.

Three-quarter length figure of the Virgin seated before a wall, the Infant Christ on her lap ; her right hand round the neck of the infant St. John, who raises his right hand to Christ ; landscape background. Panel 23½ × 16 in.

By RAPHAEL.   Lent by Col. W. CORNWALLIS WEST.

238. PORTRAIT OF A MAN.

Half-length life-size figure to right ; in brown dress and scarlet cap. Panel 23 × 18 in.

By VINCENZIO FOPPA.   Lent by ALFRED MORRISON, ESQ.

239. THE HOLY FAMILY.

Full-length figure less than life-size of the Virgin, kneeling to left in adoration over the Infant Saviour, who lies on a cushion before her ; beside them on the left is seated St. Joseph ; in the distance to right is seen the figure of the infant St. John ; buildings and landscape in the background. Panel 54 × 41¾ in.

By FRA BARTOLOMMEO.   Lent by LUDWIG MOND, ESQ.

240. ST. JOHN THE BAPTIST.

Small full-length figure of St. John, seated facing, in a rocky wilderness ; his right hand raised points to the cross ; in his left scroll ; leopard's skin over left arm and right leg. Copper 16 × 13 in. One of the copies of the celebrated large picture in the Tribune at Florence, painted by Raphael about 1518.

By GIULIO ROMANO.   Lent by the DUKE OF WESTMINSTER, K.G.

241. VISION OF EZEKIEL.

God the Father in the clouds supported by the four Evangelists and two angels. Panel 16 × 11½ in.

By RAPHAEL.   Lent by the EARL OF ASHBURNHAM.

242. CHRIST BEARING THE CROSS.

Small full-length figures ; in the centre Christ bearing the Cross, dragged and driven by soldiers and others, and followed by the Holy Women who are supporting the fainting Virgin ; in front two horsemen ; landscape background. Panel 9½ × 33 in. The centre piece of a predella painted by Raphael for the nuns of St. Antonio at Perugia. Formerly in the Orleans collection.

By RAPHAEL.   Lent by LORD WINDSOR.

243. PORTRAITS OF FERRY CARONDELET AND HIS SECRETARY.

Half-length figure, life-size, of Carondelet, in dark fur-trimmed cloak, seated at a table beneath a colonnade, holding in his left hand a letter addressed to himself at Rome ; behind him is seen the head of an attendant ; on his left sits his secretary, writing, at the same table ; on the right distant landscape and buildings. A portion of an in- scription, "NOSCE OPPORTUNITATEM," which is said to have been Carondelet's motto, can be read in the building behind him. Panel 43½ × 34 in.

Ferry, son of Jean Carondelet ; born at Malines in 1473, was elected Chanoine and Grand Archidiacre of the Chapter of Besançon in 1504 : imbibed a love for the fine arts at the Court of the Archduchess Margaret, Regent of the Netherlands ; was sent in 1510 on a mission to Rome by the Emperor Maximilian I., and whilst there enjoyed the friendship of Pope Julius II., and, it is said, of Raphael and Michelangelo ; he left Rome in 1512 for Viterbo, where he resided till 1520, and then went to Montbenoît, of which the Pope had made him the Superior in 1511 ; he died there in 1528. This picture was given by the Government of the United States of Holland to Lord Arlington, then Secretary of State for Foreign Affairs (1660–1674).

By RAPHAEL.   Lent by the DUKE OF GRAFTON, K.G.

244. HEADS OF TWO ANGELS.

Heads of two Angels, slightly over life-size, turned to the spectator and looking over their left shoulders. Canvas 13 × 20 in.

By CORREGGIO.   Lent by the EARL OF NORTHBROOK.

245. THE VIRGIN AND CHILD AND ST. JOHN.

Full-length life-size figure of the Virgin kneeling to left and lifting the veil which has covered the Infant Christ sleeping on the ground and resting against a cushion ; her left arm encircles the infant St. John, who with outstretched arms towards Christ is looking at the spectator ; landscape background with buildings, &c. Panel 51 × 43 in.

By RAPHAEL.   Lent by the DUKE OF WESTMINSTER, K.G.

246. THE ANNUNCIATION.

> Two circular medallions with half-length figures of the Virgin and St. Gabriel, on a background of arabesques. Panel 16 × 14 in.

By RAPHAEL.   Lent by the LADY SELINA HERVEY.

247. THE VISION OF ST. JEROME.

> St. John the Baptist kneeling on one knee, towards the right is pointing upwards to the vision of the Virgin with the Infant Saviour; on the right, St. Jerome lying on his back asleep. Copper 18 × 14 in.

A finished study for the large picture in the National Gallery.

By PARMIGIANO.   Lent by the DUKE OF WESTMINSTER, K.G.

248. VIRGIN AND CHILD.

> Three-quarter length figure of the Virgin seated facing, and holding the Infant Christ erect upon her knees; landscape background. Panel 20 × 14½ in.

By RAPHAEL.   Lent by the EARL OF NORTHBROOK.

249. PORTRAIT OF THE CONTESSINA MATTEI.

> Half-length life-size figure of the Contessina facing, in dark brown dress open in front, white ruff and veil. On the back of the panel is inscribed CONTESSINE D. MATTEI. DECARLIÑI VXORIS IMAGO. Panel 24 × 17 in.

By ANDREA DEL SARTO.   Lent by the DUKE OF WESTMINSTER, K.G.

250. THE NATIVITY.

> Small full-length figures of the Virgin and St. Joseph kneeling in adoration on either side of the Infant Saviour, who lies on the ground; landscape background. Panel 5 × 3½ in.

By FRA BARTOLOMMEO.   Lent by LUDWIG MOND, ESQ.

251. VIRGIN AND CHILD.

> Small three-quarter length figure of the Virgin, seated, facing, head to left, holding the Infant Saviour, Who stands on her knees. Panel 19½ × 13½ in.

By PERUGINO.   Lent by CAPT. G. L. HOLFORD, C.I.E.

252. St. Sebastian and St. Jerome.

Full-length figures of St. Sebastian bound to a tree, and St. Jerome standing to left with stone in right hand; behind him, lion; landscape background. Panels (2) 17½ × 7½ in. each.

By Perugino.   Lent by Lord Wantage, V.C.

253. Maximilian Sforza, Duke of Milan. (1491—1530.)

Half-length life-size figure to left wearing green embroidered dress and fur-trimmed sur-coat and white shirt; his left hand holds a pomander; black cap with gold medallion; red curtain and background; below, on a panel, date 1520. Panel 26½ × 20 in.

Son of Ludovico Sforza, born 1491, Duke of Milan 1512, deposed 1515, died 1530.

By Bramantino.   Lent by Capt. G. L. Holford, C.I.E.

254. Virgin and Child.

Three-quarter length figure of the Virgin seated facing, looking down at the Infant Christ on her lap; in her left hand open book. Panel 30½ × 22 in. A replica of the picture in the Berlin gallery.

By Raphael.   Lent by Charles Butler, Esq.

255. Baptism of Christ.

In a landscape with the river Jordan: full-length figure of Christ in attitude of devotion standing in the river: on the brink kneels St. John the Baptist in the act of baptizing Christ, bowl in right hand and cross in left: behind him are two angels and in the distance monks of the order of Mount Carmel and other figures: above in clouds the Holy Ghost. Panel 63½ × 48 in.

By Francia.   Lent by Her Majesty the Queen.

256. Portrait of a Young Man.

Bust in profile to left, long brown hair, black dress and white slashed vest, black cap with gold medallion. Panel 18 × 11½ in.

By Raphael.   Lent by Mrs. Austen and
                                       the Trustees of the late J. F. Austen. Esq.

257. Virgin and Child.

Small three-quarter length figure of the Virgin seated to right near the Infant Christ, Who lies asleep on a couch before her; she holds in both hands a veil which she has drawn from the Infant child. Panel 10 × 6 in. A lunette of a larger picture.

By Parmigiano.   Lent by James Knowles, Esq.

258. INFANT CHRIST AND ST. JOHN.

Small figures of Christ and St. John, as infants, seated on two cushions, embracing. Panel 8¼ × 10½ in.

By CORREGGIO.   Lent by SIR WILLIAM FARRER.

259. SAINT IN PRAYER.

Three-quarter length figure of a Saint to left in attitude of prayer, in red and blue dress. Panel 31½ × 11 in.

By PERUGINO.   Lent by LAURENCE HARDY, ESQ., M.P.

260. PORTRAIT OF A LADY.

Half-length, life-size figure, seated to left in richly embroidered and laced dress ; a veil is attached to her head by a band.   Panel 30 × 22½ in.

By GIOVANNI ANTONIO BELTRAFFIO.   Lent by ALFRED MORRISON, ESQ.

261. VIRGIN AND CHILD AND ST. JOHN.

Three-quarter-length figure of the Virgin seated to right, holding on her lap the Infant Christ, who is bending forward and caressing the infant St. John. Panel 30 × 22½ in.

By ALBERTINELLI.   Lent by ROBERT FOX, ESQ.

262. THE HOLY FAMILY AND ST. JOHN.

Full-length figure of the Virgin seated to left on a marble seat, the Infant Christ asleep on her left, His head resting on her knees ; in her right hand she holds an open book ; on the left St. John in attitude of silence ; on the right St. Joseph in meditation.   Panel 22 × 17½ in.   From a drawing by Michelangelo.

By MARCELLO VENUSTI.   Lent by COL. W. CORNWALLIS WEST.

263. ST. LUKE PAINTING THE PORTRAITS OF THE VIRGIN AND CHILD.

Small full-length figures ; in a room on the left sits St. Luke holding sketch ; before him is the Virgin seated at the foot of a bed, the Infant Christ standing on her knees ; in the background is an open doorway in which stands a man who looks at the Virgin ; beyond the doorway, landscape.   Panel 17 × 12 in.

By GIULIO ROMANO.   Lent by the DUKE OF WESTMINSTER, K.G.

264. PORTRAIT OF A YOUNG MAN PLAYING A LUTE.

Three-quarter length portrait of a young man with long brown hair, seated on a wall, and playing a lute : green dress, red coat, and black cap ; landscape with mountains in the background ; on the left a group of small figures representing the triumph of Love ; and on the right Apollo and Daphne. Panel 39 × 28½ in.

By FRANCESCO UBERTINI   Lent by CHARLES BUTLER, ESQ.
(IL BACCHIACCA.)

265. THE MASS OF ST. GREGORY.

St. Gregory in rich ecclesiastical robes stands between deacon and sub-deacon before an altar, holding the sacred host in his two hands ; before him is a vision of the risen
· Christ under an arch with landscape background ; on either side of the altar stands an angel holding a taper and swinging a censer ; on the altar are the Papal tiara, a missal, the vessels and two lighted candles. Signed and dated 1501. Panel transferred to Canvas 76½ × 74½ in.
This picture is mentioned by Vasari as being in his day in the Church of Santo Spirito at Florence, but incorrectly attributed by him to Raffaellino del Garbo. Another picture signed by Karli is in the Corsini Palace at Florence.

By RAFFAELLO KARLI.

266. ST. MARY MAGDALEN.

Life-size three-quarter length figure of St. Mary Magdalen seated facing, holding a vase in her right hand ; red dress with large sleeves. Perhaps a portrait of the artist's wife. Panel 36 × 27 in.

By ANDREA DEL SARTO.   Lent by CHARLES BUTLER, ESQ.

DRAWINGS.

267. HERCULES AND ANTÆUS.
By LUCA SIGNORELLI.   Lent by HER MAJESTY THE QUEEN.

268. STUDY FOR THE FIGURE OF POETRY. On the ceiling of the Camera della Segnatura.
By RAPHAEL.   Lent by HER MAJESTY THE QUEEN.

269. STUDY OF A CHILD'S HEAD.
By LIONARDO DA VINCI.   Lent by HER MAJESTY THE QUEEN.

E

270. SKETCH FOR THE FIGURE OF CHRIST. A design for the Resurrection.

By MICHELANGELO.   Lent by HER MAJESTY THE QUEEN.

271. STUDY OF A HEAD. On the back are studies for figures for the frescoes in the Chapel of San Lorenzo in the Vatican.

By FRA ANGELICO.   Lent by HER MAJESTY THE QUEEN.

272. STUDIES OF HEADS OF JUDAS AND THREE OTHER APOSTLES FOR THE FRESCO OF THE LAST SUPPER.   •

By LIONARDO DA VINCI.   Lent by Dr. J. P. RICHTER.

273. STUDY FOR THE ARMOUR OF THE FIGURE OF ST. MICHAEL in the Holy Family, in the National Gallery.

By PERUGINO.   Lent by HER MAJESTY THE QUEEN.

274. ROMAN SOLDIERS. A group of four men in Roman costume, bistre drawing.

By POLIDORO DA CARAVAGGIO.   Lent by HER MAJESTY THE QUEEN.

275. STUDY FOR THE CARTOON OF THE CHARGE TO ST. PETER.

By RAPHAEL.   Lent by HER MAJESTY THE QUEEN.

276. PORTRAIT OF A YOUNG MAN. Silver-point drawing.

By LORENZO DI CREDI.   Lent by ALFRED MORRISON, ESQ.

277. STUDY FOR THE HEAD OF AN APOSTLE FOR THE FRESCO OF THE LAST SUPPER.

By LIONARDO DA VINCI.   Lent by HER MAJESTY THE QUEEN.

278. STUDY FOR A HEAD.

By FRA ANGELICO.   Lent by HER MAJESTY THE QUEEN.

279. THE "SHOOTERS AT A MARK."
By MICHELANGELO.   Lent by HER MAJESTY THE QUEEN.

280. THE "BACCHANALE DEI PUTTI."
By MICHELANGELO.   Lent by HER MAJESTY THE QUEEN.

281. STUDY FOR THE HEAD OF ST. ANNE IN THE HOLY FAMILY IN THE
            LOUVRE.
By LIONARDO DA VINCI.   Lent by HER MAJESTY THE QUEEN.

282. STUDY OF AN ANGEL IN THE FRESCO OF THE TEMPTATION OF
            ST. ANTHONY IN THE APPARTAMENTI BORGIA IN THE
            VATICAN.
By PINTURICCHIO.   Lent by HER MAJESTY THE QUEEN.

WEST GALLERY.

WORKS OF ART.

CASE A.

ECCLESIASTICAL PLATE AND ORNAMENTS.

283. PROCESSIONAL CRUCIFIX, in silver.

Lent by CHARLES BUTLER, ESQ.

284. THURIBLE of copper gilt pierced and ornamented with figures and scroll foliage with the figures of Ananias, Azarias, and Misael. This Thurible was brought from a church at Pavia. 12th century.

Lent by the RIGHT REV. the BISHOP OF SOUTHWARK.

285. SILVER POMANDER OR PERFUME BURNER.

Lent by the RIGHT REV. the BISHOP OF SOUTHWARK.

286. PAX, silver-gilt, enamelled and jewelled.

Lent by HENRY WAGNER, ESQ.

287. INCENSE BOAT AND SPOON. An engraved panel, of cusped ogee quatrefoil form, formerly covered the present engraving of a Bishop. From the Magniac collection.

Lent by JAMES GURNEY, ESQ.

288. CHALICE in bronze gilt, inlaid with figures in translucent enamel. '

Lent by CHARLES BUTLER, ESQ.

289. CHALICE, gilt metal, globular knop and six-lobed repoussé base. Circ. 1440.

Lent by the BIRMINGHAM MUSEUM AND ART GALLERY.

290. PAX, bronze gilt frame with silver plaque ; the figures of the Saviour and angels are in high relief.

> Lent by the BIRMINGHAM MUSEUM AND ART GALLERY.

291. CHASED SILVER PLAQUE ; repoussé. The figure of the Saviour in bold relief, with heads of angels and clouds in the background.

> Lent by WILLIAM BOORE, ESQ.

292. TORTOISE-SHELL CABINET, with enamelled silver plaques.

> Lent by MRS. COWELL.

293. CHALICE, copper gilt, chased and engraved, centre of stem enriched with knobs which contained six medallions in champlevé enamel. From the Pirri Collection. 1400.

> Lent by the BIRMINGHAM MUSEUM AND ART GALLERY.

294 CASKET in wood and brass work ; an ivory figure in centre of each panel.

> Lent by CHARLES BUTLER, ESQ.

295. A GILDED BRONZE PAX—Christ in the tomb,

> Lent by the RIGHT REV. the BISHOP OF PORTSMOUTH.

296. RELIQUARY, bronze gilt, hexagonal, of gothic design with chased and pierced spires, on shaped foot.

> Lent by CHARLES BUTLER, ESQ.

297. DISH, silver gilt with embossed border of nymphs, tritons, &c.

> Lent by CHARLES BRINSLEY MARLAY, ESQ.

298. COPPER GILT CANDLESTICK.

> Lent by the BIRMINGHAM MUSEUM AND ART GALLERY.

299. THE END OF A CHASSE, copper repoussé work.

> Lent by the Right Rev. the BISHOP OF PORTSMOUTH.

300. PAX, bronze gilt. The Virgin and Child ; the Virgin robed in tunic and mantle.

> Lent by T. WHITCOMBE GREENE, ESQ.

---

301. PAX, bronze gilt.

Lent by C. FAIRFAX MURRAY, ESQ.

302. SILVER GILT CHALICE. The work of Bartolomeo d'Atri and supposed to have belonged to Boniface VIII., 1294-1303. The upper part of the foot is wrought with vine leaves, and around it is the inscription in niello—"Antonius Sabini Notaris Fecit me Fieri a Magistro Bartolomeo Ser. Pauli De Atri." 14th century.

Lent by the Right Rev. the BISHOP OF SOUTHWARK.

303. SUPER-ALTAR OR PORTABLE ALTAR. The slab is of oriental jasper let into oak both chased in silver. Border elaborately ornamented with scrolls, some of which are fitted with niello. At the four corners are the elements symbolised as youthful virgins, viz. : Fire, Water, Earth, and Air. In the middle of the north border stands the Agnus Dei ; to the right St. Gabriel holding a long sceptre ; on the left St. Michael. In the centre of the south border is a nimbed dove. This piece of church furniture is considered to be one of the finest examples now extant, and once belonged to Cardinal Bessarion, who bequeathed it to the Abbey of Avellanna in Gubbio. When the French occupied Italy the Abbot sold it to Count Cicognara. It was eventually bequeathed to St. George's Cathedral by the Rev. Dr. Rock. Late 12th century.

Lent by the Right Rev. the BISHOP OF SOUTHWARK.

304. HOLY WATER STOUP, copper, pierced and hammered.

Lent by the Right Rev. the BISHOP OF PORTSMOUTH.

305. CHALICE in bronze gilt, on the knop busts in translucent enamel.

Lent by CHARLES BUTLER, ESQ.

306. COLLECTION BOX in wood, with designs in relief. From the Spitzer Collection. 16th century.

Lent by the BIRMINGHAM MUSEUM AND ART GALLERY.

307. JEWELLERY BOX in stamped leather, painted.

Lent by the BIRMINGHAM MUSEUM AND ART GALLERY.

308. SILVER CIBORIUM, with gilt bronze stand and cover. Late 16th century.

Lent by C. E. HARRIS, ESQ.

309. SILVER ORNAMENT of triangular form, with cherubs at the angles, and drapery ; repoussé work.

Lent by JAMES GURNEY, ESQ.

310. A SILVER HAND-BELL of Pope Clement VII., chased with masks and foliage, male and female figures, animals, &c., in high relief. The ring forming the handle is the emblem of Giulio de' Medici (Clement VII).

Lent by C. J. JACKSON, ESQ.

311. CHALICE, silver gilt, the base and stem are embellished with medallions of the Crucifixion, the Virgin, and Saints in translucent enamel.

Lent by HENRY WILLETT, ESQ.

312. PAIR OF BURETTES, mounted in gilt metal. 16th century. From the Spitzer collection.

Lent by FREDERICK DAVIS, ESQ

313. PAX, bronze gilt.

Lent by C. FAIRFAX-MURRAY, ESQ.

314. CHALICE, silver gilt with enamelled bosses on knop.

Lent by CAPTAIN H. B. MURRAY.

315. CHALICE, silver gilt, with engraved floral patterns on foot and bowl.

Lent by CAPTAIN H. B. MURRAY.

316. SMALL SUPER-ALTAR, with slab of porphyry let into an oak-frame ; the back is of copper gilt, with repoussé fleurs de lis pattern. 12th century. Formerly in the possession of Dr. Rock.

Lent by the RIGHT REV. THE BISHOP OF SOUTHWARK.

317. CASKET, bearing the arms of the Medici family, of elaborately embossed and gilt leather, with the original lock, and encased with wrought iron bands.

Lent by MRS. P. C. HARDWICK.

318. CHALICE of silver, with foot of repoussé work ; medallion and flowers.

Lent by CHARLES BRINSLEY MARLAY, ESQ.

319. PAX in bronze gilt and silver niello, representing the Adoration of the Shepherds 15th century. From the Spitzer collection, No. 336.

Lent by FREDERICK DAVIS, ESQ:

320. CASKET, covered with velvet, and with gilt mountings, the front ornamented with two gilt medallions with busts.

Lent by the HON. W. F. B. MASSEY MAINWARING.

321. PAX, bronze gilt ; the Virgin and Child surrounded by angels.

Lent by T. WHITCOMBE GREENE, ESQ.

322. RELIQUARY, hexagonal of gothic design with chased and pierced spires on shaped foot.

Lent by CHARLES BUTLER, ESQ.

323. ROCK CRYSTAL CASKET, decorated with spiral rock crystal columns with silver capitals and bases. The frame is ornamented with minutely painted leaves and arabesque patterns, birds and animals, to imitate damascening in gold on iron. It is inlaid with rock crystal plaques. 16th century.

Lent by ALFRED DE ROTHSCHILD, ESQ.

324. CHALICE ; bowl of silver, gilt stem, the base of copper gilt with floral border. 15th century.

Lent by the BIRMINGHAM MUSEUM AND ART GALLERY.

325. SMALL CABINET of ebony. The sides mounted with temples, boys, lions, masks of ormolu and female figures in ivory. The top formed of a large metal plaque chased with figures, fitted with drawers, ivory figures, &c., in relief.

Lent by CHARLES BUTLER, ESQ.

326. DAMASCENED BOX, representing hunting scenes.

Lent by CHARLES BUTLER, ESQ.

PAPAL AND OTHER RINGS OF INVESTITURE.

Exhibited by A. W. Franks, Esq., C.B.

[IN CASE C.]

327. BRONZE gilt with cloisonné enamels. From Corfu.

328. BRONZE gilt with pounced ornaments, Papal emblems, &c.

329. BRONZE gilt, chased. Pope Clement VI., 1342–1352.

330. BRONZE gilt, pounced ornament. Anti-Pope Benedict XII–XIII., 1394-1417.

331. BRONZE gilt and chased. Eugenius IV. 1431-1447.

332. BRONZE gilt and chased. Pope Paul II. 1464-1471.

333. BRONZE gilt and chased. Innocent VIII. 1484-1492.

334. BRONZE, once gilt ; signet. Arms of the Medici.

335. BRONZE, gilt and chased. Biscia of the Visconti.

336. BRONZE gilt and chased ; of a Pope Pius.

337. BRONZE gilt and chased ; fleurs de lis and suns.

338. BRONZE gilt and chased, probably Episcopal.

339. PAPAL RING, bronze gilt, with evangelistic symbols, tiara and cross keys.

340. PAPAL RING, probably of Nicholas V. 1447—1455.

CASE B.

BRONZES AND PLAQUETTES.

BRONZES LENT BY H. PFUNGST, ESQ.

345. NUDE RECLINING FEMALE FIGURE. A reduced copy of Michelangelo's figure of Evening, being one of the recumbent figures supporting the tomb of Lorenzo de' Medici (Il Penseroso). Florentine ; middle 16th century.

346. CANDLESTICK. Boy supporting with left arm a branch terminating in vase-shaped nozzle and holding cup in right hand. 16th century.

347. INKSTAND. Boy seated astride a large shell, forming an inkstand, and holding cornucopia ; triangular base. Late 15th or early 16th century.

348. VESTAL VIRGIN holding patera. 16th century.

349. LAMP. Boy in short shirt carrying large shell on his back. School of Verrocchio; late 15th or early 16th century.

350. LION walking. Florentine, School of Donatello ; middle of 15th century.

351. CUPID, left hand resting on shield, right supporting cornucopia. North Italian ; late 15th or early 16th century.

352. TIME or CHRONOS holding hour-glass extended in right hand, left resting on scythe. Possibly adapted from the antique. Early 16th century.

353. CENTAUR carrying off a woman (Nessus and Dejanira). Florentine ; latter half of 16th century.

354. TRITON riding on a Tortoise and blowing a conch shell—stand for a salt cellar. Gilt. 16th century.

355. INK-STAND. A sea monster terminating in a human head supporting an open shell in his mouth (receptacle for the ink) and a similar shell on his back. Early 16th century.

356. LAMP. A satyr seated and blowing a long conch-shell terminating in a grotesque human head, supported by his feet. Latter half of 15th century.

357. INK-STAND. On a circular base, an Equestrian Figure (Marcus Aurelius) ; to right a shell (for ink). Latter half of 15th century.

358. YOUTHFUL BACCHUS with leopard. Latter half of 15th century.

359. YOUNG HERCULES resting on club ; lion's skin hanging from his shoulders, the head of the lion in form of human face. Attributed to Andrea del Verrocchio. Florentine ; latter half of 15th century. .

360. INK-STAND AND LAMP. Kneeling figure of Satyr, right hand supporting lamp, ornamented with sun and stars ; left resting on a tub (receptacle for the ink) placed on bed of fruit, flowers, &c., from which creep snakes. Base decorated with classical ornaments in low relief. School of "Il Riccio"; latter half of 15th century.

361. YOUNG DAVID, standing on head of Goliath, right hand resting on sword ; left grasping satchel suspended from his shoulders. The features of David resemble those of Lorenzo de' Medici.   School of Donatello. Florentine ; middle of 15th century.

362. HERCULES CAPTURING CERBERUS. Probably Florentine work of the middle of the 16th century.

363. CUPID stretching out, as if he had shot an arrow. Attributed to Donatello. Florentine ; middle of 15th century.

364. WRITING CASE, a box supported on four caryatid feet. The cover is ornamented with two Cupids supporting shield of arms with wreath border. On the front and back are centaurs carrying off women, and on each side the head of Medusa. Roman ?   Attributed to Ambrogio Foppa, called "Caradosso" ; end of 15th century.

365. WRITING CASE, an oblong box supported by four dolphins. On lid is an allegorical figure of Slander (attributed to "Il Riccio"), and in front and at back, head of Bacchante in alto relievo (by "Moderno"). North Italian ; late 15th century.

366. VULCAN forging spear-head on anvil ; the god represented with a wooden leg. Latter half of 16th century.

367. YOUTH drawing a thorn from his foot ; after the antique. Florentine ; latter half of the 15th century.

368. FEMALE SATYR holding shell from which young faun is drinking. Late 15th or early 16th century. The base, on which is an ewer and a goat, appears to be of later date. The whole is chased.

369. EQUESTRIAN FIGURE of a warrior, right arm raised, left hand holding the reins. North Italian ; late 15th or early 16th century.

370. DOOR-HANDLE. A nude female figure with long flowing hair and outspread wings ; body terminating in two twisted snake-like tails.   School of "Il Riccio." Italian ; latter half of 15th century.

371. INKSTAND. Youth, wearing sheepskin, supporting small tub on his arms; legs crossed. Italian ; School of Verrocchio ; middle 15th century.

372. ST. JEROME praying, holding a stone in his right hand. North Italian ; middle of 15th century.

373. LAMP. Head of Satyr, with beard formed of fig-leaves ; mouth open and tongue protruding. Latter half of 15th century.

374. ST. MICHAEL standing on dragon, holding sword in right hand and scales in left. School of Donatello. Middle of 15th century.

375. INKSTAND AND COVER. Triangular in shape ; decorated with classical ornaments in low relief and supported by scrolls ending in Lion's claws. The cover ornamented with acanthus leaves ending in a knot formed by the same. Latter half of 15th century.

BRONZE PLAQUETTES LENT BY J. P. HESELTINE, ESQ.

376. FIGURE CARRYING COLUMN. By Giulio della Torre.

377. CHRIST, St. Thomas, and other Apostles.

378. VENUS AND CUPID. By Giulio della Torre.

379. VIRGIN AND CHILD.

380. HERCULES AND ANTÆUS. By Moderno.

381. HERCULES STRANGLING LION.

382. SACRIFICIAL SCENE. By Riccio.

383. HORSEMAN KILLING BOAR.

384. VENUS AND DIVINITIES. Signed 10 FF. (Giovanni Corniole.)

385. BACCHUS. Half-length figure.

386. VENUS AND SATYRS.

387. ST. GEORGE AND THE DRAGON.

388. VIRGIN AND CHILD (*a Par*). By Moderno.

389. DESCENT FROM THE CROSS.

390. VIRGIN AND CHILD WITH SAINTS. By Moderno.

391. HERCULES STRANGLING LION. By Moderno.

392. HERCULES STRANGLING SERPENTS.

393. WARRIORS AND OTHERS. Ornament for the hilt of a sword.

394. ST. JEROME AND THE LION. By Ulocrino.

395. PRESENTATION IN THE TEMPLE. By Moderno.

396. VIRGIN AND CHILD WITH CHERUBIM. By Modern

397. HERCULES AND NESSUS. By Moderno.

398. VENUS AND MARS. By Moderno.

399. HERCULES SLAYING NESSUS. By Moderno.

400. ST. SEBASTIAN.

401. THE FLAGELLATION. By Pollaiulo.

402. NYMPH AND SATYR.

403. TWO WARRIORS. A piece to be worn in the hat.

CASE C.

PERSONAL ORNAMENTS, &c.

404. LARGE ROCK CRYSTAL VASE. 16th century. Richly engraved in arabesques. It is mounted in gold enamel; the handle represents a winged dragon and the lip an eagle's head. The whole rests on a rock crystal gold-mounted stem. The gold enamel work is by Charles Duron of Paris.

Lent by FREDERICK DAVIS, ESQ.

405. ROCK CRYSTAL VASE, carved as an Ostrich; partly mounted in silver gilt. The ornaments are in enamelled gold.

Lent by FREDERICK DAVIS, ESQ.

406. HANAPIN OF ROCK CRYSTAL. From the Spitzer collection.

Lent by MISS ETHEL FOSTER.

407. PENDANT ENSEIGNE or RELIQUARY, consisting of a cylindrical portion of an arm-bone and mounted in a framework formed of three hoops of gold, set with gems, and elaborately enriched with translucent enamels of the richest colours. The bone appears in the intervals of these decorations; at each extremity is a convex circular plate, exquisitely enamelled, attached by a hinge so as to close the open end of the piece of bone and forming the lid of a small receptacle, in which a scented pastille was enclosed, probably as a precaution against any unpleasant odour from the relic. Upon the cylinder is affixed, on a richly jewelled base, a crucifix, with figures of the Virgin and St. John. The figures are in full relief (*lavoro di piastra*), the garments and all details elaborately enamelled. On the reverse of the cross appear the emblems of the Passion, and beneath is a medallion delicately painted, representing the Fall. To the upper side of the framework, ending the cylinder, are attached two chains, richly jewelled at intervals, uniting in an arched ornament at top, set with diamonds and rubies, and having a ring by which the jewel might be suspended. To the lower side of the cylinder it appears that three pendants, now lost, were attached. This reliquary is perhaps unique in the beauty of the varied hues of the enamels, for the most part translucent on relief, with which it is everywhere enriched, and also in the perfection of the skill of the goldsmith. It may be assigned to the commencement of the 16th century.

This reliquary is traditionally said to have belonged to Catherine of Braganza, and to have been given by her to the family of the Comptons of Hartpury, county Gloucester.

Lent by WILLIAM BOORE, ESQ.

408. JEWEL, in form of a triton. 16th century.

Lent by the MARQUESS OF CLANRIKARDE.

409. ROCK CRYSTAL CUP, engraved, with detached handle, in the form of the chimæra. 16th century.

Lent by MESSRS. DURLACHER BROS.

410. PAIR OF FIVE DROP EARRINGS.

Lent by the MISSES LOUISA AND LUCY COHEN.

411. ENAMELLED GOLD NECKLACE AND PENDANT of Cellini work, set with pearls, rubies, and diamonds. Seated figures in enamel on pendant.

Lent by CAPTAIN H. NAYLOR LEYLAND, M.P.

412. PENDANT JEWEL of gold decorated with enamel and set with jewels. It is in the form of a fish, the body enamelled white, and having large rubies, &c., on both sides. On its back is a small figure of a man with club and buckler. It is suspended by a chain with enamelled points and a pendant pearl.

Lent by BARON FERDINAND DE ROTHSCHILD, M.P.

413. GOLD ENAMELLED PENDANT JEWEL representing a hippocamp, with a figure of a young woman ; in her hand is a trident. The body of the animal is inlaid with thirteen emeralds. The whole is suspended from a gold enamelled chain enriched with pearls. From the Debruge and Londesborough collections.

Lent by BARON FERDINAND DE ROTHSCHILD, M.P.

414. GOLD ENAMELLED PENDANT JEWEL of a marine horse suspended from a chain set with rubies and emeralds ; the body of the animal is formed of a large baroque pearl ; the head is of white enamel. Five pearls are suspended from the jewel, which is also decorated with surface enamelling. From the Londesborough collection.

Lent by BARON FERDINAND DE ROTHSCHILD, M.P.

415. PENDANT JEWEL of a mermaid holding a comb of gold. The chain for suspension is decorated with translucent enamel and enriched by diamonds and emeralds.

The headdress is set with large emeralds ; the bands crossing the breast and arms are enamelled sapphire blue ; a circular ornament covers the body and is enriched with emeralds and coloured enamels—this forms a lid to the hollow body of the figure. The tail is covered with enamels in red, green and purple, set with emeralds, as also is the back of the figure.

Lent by BARON FERDINAND DE ROTHSCHILD, M.P.

416. PENDANT JEWEL of gold, richly decorated with translucent enamels and set with rubies. It is of semi-oviform shape, pierced with strap work on the under side, which is enamelled red, white, &c., with a pendant pearl. The upper surface is engraved with flowers, filled with translucent enamel and has a figure of a parrot, enamelled green and set with rubies. It is suspended from three chains.

Lent by BARON FERDINAND DE ROTHSCHILD, M.P.

417. SILVER-GILT FOOT OR STEM for a cup. The foot is covered with scroll work, and three heads in bold relief. On the stem three heads of angels and garlands of flowers. By Cellini.

Lent by WILLIAM BOORE, ESQ.

418. POMANDER of silver-gilt, for a variety of perfumes ; on the foot the arms of a cardinal. 16th century.

Lent by C. H. READ, ESQ.

419. POMANDER of similar form and make.

Lent by C. H. READ, ESQ.

420. SMALL BOTTLE, chased with scrolls and cherubs' heads, with medallion of the Flagellation, &c.

Lent by JAMES GURNEY, ESQ.

421. AMBER CASKET richly carved with arabesque ornaments, and mounted at sides with caryatides in ivory and enamelled. The lid is surmounted by a snail, also of amber and enamelled, astride of which is a small figure of a boy holding a spear 16th century.

Lent by The HON. W. F. B. MASSEY-MAINWARING.

422. SMALL STEEL CABINET, repoussé, with figures, masks, grotesques, and ornaments damascened in gold and silver. Milanese. 16th century.

Lent by DAVID CURRIE, ESQ.

JEWELLERY AND FINGER RINGS. LENT BY FREDERICK DAVIS, ESQ.

423. DEVOTIONAL PENDANT formed of plaques of rock crystal mounted in gold richly enamelled. The subjects are painted on the back of the crystal : on one side the Agony in the Garden, on the other the Resurrection. From the Spitzer collection, No. 2105. 16th century.

424. JEWELLED PENDANT of gold enamelled, and set with rubies, emeralds and pearls. On the top a dog formed of a baroque pearl. From the Spitzer collection, No. 1841. 16th century.

425. FINGER RING, gold, set with rough sapphire ; at the back clasped hands and inscription on the hoop. From the Spitzer collection, No. 1884. 13th century.

426. A FINGER RING. Silver gilt, set with a ruby between two figures of lions in full relief. From the Spitzer collection, No. 1885. Early 15th century.

427. FINGER RING OF GOLD, richly enamelled and chased ; quatrefoil bezel set with a ruby. From the Spitzer collection, No. 1889.

428. FINGER RING OF GOLD, richly enamelled and chased ; oblong bezel set with a ruby and an emerald. From the Spitzer collection, No. 1892. 16th century.

429. FINGER RING OF GOLD, richly enamelled and chased ; cruciform bezel set with six rubies and a pyramidal diamond for writing on glass. From the Spitzer collection, No. 1898. 16th century.

430. FINGER RING OF GOLD, with square bezel set with a turquoise. From the Spitzer collection, No. 1917. 16th century.

431. FINGER RING OF GOLD, with high square bezel set with a ruby and an emerald. From the Spitzer collection, No. 1919. 16th century.

432. FINGER RING OF GOLD, enamelled and chased, the bezel in form of a lion ; clasped hand at back. From the Spitzer collection, No. 1921. 16th century.

433. FINGER RING OF GOLD, enamelled with high square bezel set with a ruby and clasped by two hands. From the Spitzer collection, No. 1941. 16th century.

434. DOUBLE FINGER RING of gold richly enamelled, soldered together; each with a quatrefoil bezel, set with a ruby and a diamond. From the Spitzer collection, No. 1,901. 16th century.

435. FINGER RING of gold, enamelled and chased, square bezel set with a ruby. From the Spitzer collection, No. 1,907. 16th century.

436. FINGER RING of gold set with a ruby. From the Spitzer collection, No. 1,909. 16th century.

437. FINGER RING of gold set with a ruby. From the Spitzer collection, No. 1911. 16th century.

438. PENDANT JEWEL, designed as a mermaid, with diamond necklet. The front of the body is formed of a baroque pearl: the back of chased gold: the tail set with emeralds. 16th century.
Lent by ALFRED DE ROTHSCHILD, ESQ.

439. SMALL JEWEL OF CHASED GOLD, representing a lion holding an antelope between its paws. The lion's back is formed of a baroque pearl. 16th century.
Lent by ALFRED DE ROTHSCHILD, ESQ.

440. SMALL JEWEL in the form of a dog sitting on its haunches. The body is formed of a baroque pearl; round its neck is a collar studded with diamonds. 16th century.
Lent by ALFRED DE ROTHSCHILD, ESQ.

441. A JEWEL of enamelled gold in the form of a parrot with a ruby and diamond collar and flowers composed of rubies. The body of the bird is formed of a baroque pearl. 16th century.
Lent by ALFRED DE ROTHSCHILD, ESQ.

442. GOLD SPOON AND FORK. One handle serving for both. The handle is fluted and inscribed with two bands, one of which is chased with masks and fruit, the other with Cupid's head, scrolls and flowers. At the top is a chased ball upon which a female figure kneels. The front is decorated with dolphins, St. George and the Dragon, &c. 16th century.
Lent by ALFRED DE ROTHSCHILD, ESQ.

443. PENDANT JEWEL OF ENAMELLED GOLD ; designed as a mermaid ; part of the body is formed of a pearl, the scales on the back are of blue enamel, and the tail set with rubies and emeralds. 16th century.

Lent by ALFRED DE ROTHSCHILD, ESQ.

FINGER RINGS, CAMEOS, &c. LENT BY J. LUMSDEN PROPERT,
ESQ., M.D.,

444. A SAINT RECLINING. Large carving in onyx.

445. TWO PIECES of minutely carved boxwood, illustrating Hercules, Amorini, &c.

446. GROUP IN BOX-WOOD, St. Michael and Satan, on ebony pedestal.

447. FIGURE OF HEBE IN BOX-WOOD, set in a locket, with enamelled gold ornament.

448. SMALL FIGURE OF ST. FRANCIS, carved in box-wood.

449. WAX PORTRAIT of a gentleman, in bronze gilt case.

450. WAX PORTRAIT of a gentleman, in bronze gilt case.

451. THE FARNESE HERCULES, in miniature. Carved in soapstone. Florentine. 16th century.

452. GOLD RING. Head of Bacchus. Onyx cameo.

453. GOLD RING. Victory in a quadriga. Onyx cameo.

454. GOLD RING. Bust of Philosopher. Onyx cameo.

455. GOLD RING. Bust of Mars. Emerald cameo.

456. GOLD RING. A ball. Onyx cameo.

457. GOLD AND ENAMEL RING. A mask with diamond eyes.

458. GOLD AND ENAMEL RING, set with an emerald.

459. TRIPLE GOLD AND ENAMEL RING, set with rubies.

460. GOLD AND ENAMEL RING. Badge of the Knights of Malta.

F 2

461. GOLD AND ENAMEL Betrothal Ring.

462. CARVED IVORY JEWEL, with pearls.   Satyr and Nymph.

463. GOLD RELIQUAIRE, with onyx cameo of Christ.

464. KNIFE AND FORK.   Crystal handles, gold enamel tips of monkey and fruit.

465. GOLD AND ENAMEL JEWEL.   Ship in full sail.

466. ONYX CAMEO.   A satyr.

467. ONYX CAMEO.   Jupiter Ammon.

468. ONYX CAMEO.   Head of Hercules.

469. ONYX CAMEO.   Ganymede and the Eagle.

470. FEMALE BUST on bloodstone back, carved from various stones.

471. SHELL CAMEO.   Descent of the Holy Ghost.

472. SHELL CAMEO.   A battle.

473. AMETHYST INTAGLIO.   A bearded head.

---

474. A ROCK CRYSTAL CUP.
> Lent by the DUKE OF ST. ALBANS.

475. BELT with silver mounts enamelled and nielloed with arms and initials " L.B." and motto " Con el Tempo."   Silversmith's mark, a horse.
> Lent by A. W. FRANKS, ESQ., C.B.

476. RING of Pope Martin V.   Set with a crystal and bearing the Colonna arms.
> Lent by CHARLES BUTLER, ESQ.

477. CRYSTAL INKSTAND.   Lent by CHARLES BUTLER, ESQ.

478. CASKET in gesso.   Lent by CHARLES BUTLER, ESQ.

CASE D.

BRONZES, CRYSTALS, &c.

486. BRONZE MEDAL OF SIGISMONDO MALATESTA, Lord of Rimini (Anno 1446.) By Matteo di Pasti.
Lent by H. MONTAGU, ESQ.

487. BRONZE MEDAL OF ISOTTA ATTI DA RIMINI, wife of Sigismondo Malatesta. By Matteo di Pasti.
Lent by H. MONTAGU, ESQ.

488. BRONZE MEDAL OF COSIMO DE' MEDICI. Attributed to Nicolo Fiorentino.
Lent by H. MONTAGU, ESQ.

489. BRONZE MEDAL with portrait of Lorenzo de' Medici, " Il Magnifico " 1448-1492. By Sangallo.
Lent by J. H. FITZHENRY, ESQ.

490. BRONZE PLAQUE with Gorgon's Head. Part of the Donatello Inkstand. From the Spitzer collection.
Lent by J. H. FITZHENRY, ESQ.

KEYS. LENT BY T. WHITCOMBE GREENE, ESQ.

491. STEEL KEY. Handle formed by dolphins. 16th century.

492. STEEL KEY. The handle decorated with griffins surrounded with masks. 16th century.

493. STEEL KEY, with fluted stem. The handle formed by two dolphins. 16th century.

494. STEEL KEY of a Cassone or Marriage Coffer. The handle decorated with busts and foliage supporting a heart. 16th century.

495. STEEL KEY. Gilt, with fluted stem. 16th century.

496. STEEL KEY. Handle decorated with griffins interlaced. 16th century.

497. STEEL KEY. The handle formed in open work with female busts, foliage, &c. supporting an armorial lion beneath coronet and fleurs de lis.   16th century.

498. STEEL KEY. Handle formed of three grotesque winged figures.   16th century.

499. STEEL KEY. The handle decorated with masks, dolphins, and grotesque figures supporting a basket of fruit.   16th century.

500. SLAB OF BLOODSTONE, painted with the Flagellation.   Florentine.   16th century.

Lent by J. LUMSDEN PROPERT, ESQ., M.D.

501. NIELLO ON SILVER. The Temptation of Adam, copied from the Raphael fresco in the Loggia of the Vatican.

Lent by J. LUMSDEN PROPERT, ESQ., M.D.

502. WAX PORTRAIT of a Florentine Lady.

Lent by J. LUMSDEN PROPERT, ESQ., M.D.

503. CRYSTAL, Head of St. Charles Borromeo.   1538-1594.

Lent by H. WILLETT, ESQ.

504. TWO CRYSTALS, representing Jupiter and Juno.

Lent by H. WILLETT, ESQ.

505. THE ADORATION OF THE MAGI.   Painted on crystal.

Lent by the RIGHT HON. SIR HENRY AUSTIN LAYARD, G.C.B.

506. BOXWOOD HANDLE, representing Hercules with club and lion's skin.

Lent by T. FOSTER SHATTOCK, ESQ.

507. BOXWOOD HANDLE for a knife.   Representing Judith.

Lent by T. FOSTER SHATTOCK, ESQ.

508 STEEL GIPCIÈRE or purse mount.

Lent by T. FOSTER SHATTOCK, ESQ.

509. BRONZE PLAQUETTE, representing a sacrifice.   15th century.

Lent by ISAAC FALCKE, ESQ.

510. STEEL KEY, with the Medici Arms.

Lent by T. FOSTER SHATTOCK, ESQ.

511. BRONZE OVAL PLAQUE, with female bust.

Lent by T. FOSTER SHATTOCK, ESQ.

512. SILVER PIERCED BROOCH, ornamented with heads and flowers.

Lent by T. FOSTER SHATTOCK, ESQ

513. SILVER SCENT CASE.

Lent by T. FOSTER SHATTOCK, ESQ.

514. STEEL KEY composed of fantastic winged caryatides, masks, dolphins, &c. ; open work, and resting upon a Corinthian column. 16th century. From Baron Sellière's Collection.

Lent by DAVID M. CURRIE, ESQ.

515. SMALL FRAME OF CHESTNUT WOOD, carved with winged figures, cherubs' heads, flowers, &c. 16th century.

Lent by DAVID M. CURRIE, ESQ.

516. BRONZE PLAQUETTE. A Lady at her toilet, with two female attendants, and a child holding a Mirror. By Antonio Abondio.

Lent by DAVID M. CURRIE, ESQ.

517. BRONZE PLAQUE. The Virgin and Child enthroned, surrounded by Angels and Amorini, holding garlands of flowers. 15th century.

Lent by DAVID M. CURRIE, ESQ.

518. BRONZE PLAQUETTE. St. Jerome. 15th century.

Lent by DAVID M. CURRIE, ESQ

519. BRONZE PLAQUETTE. The Battle of the Amazons. Signed, Ioannes di Bernardi.

Lent by DAVID M. CURRIE, ESQ.

520. BRONZE PLAQUETTE. Lucretia.

Lent by DAVID M. CURRIE, ESQ

521. BRONZE PLAQUETTE. The Good Samaritan.

Lent Ly DAVID M. CURRIE, ESQ.

---

522. SMALL MIRROR OF STEEL, the back and front damascened with ornaments in gold and silver ; at the top a silver gilt mask.   Milanese work of the 16th century.

Lent by DAVID M. CURRIE, ESQ.

523. BRONZE PLAQUETTE, chased in high relief with figures of Boys gathering grapes, silvered and gilt.   16th century.

Lent by DAVID M. CURRIE, ESQ.

524. PLAQUETTE.   St. John.   15th century.

Lent by DAVID M. CURRIE, ESQ.

525. SMALL STEEL PLAQUETTE, with figure of Apollo embossed in high relief on a ground damascened with gold.   16th century.

Lent by DAVID M. CURRIE, ESQ.

526. SMALL KNIFE.   The handle of mother-of-pearl and steel, terminating in a column and a helmeted head.   16th century.

Lent by DAVID M. CURRIE, ESQ.

527. KNIFE AND FORK, the handles formed of niello work and silver gilt, chased with masks and flowers.   16th century.

Lent by DAVID M. CURRIE, ESQ.

528. SMALL BOXWOOD MIRROR FRAME carved with satyrs, masks, griffins, fruit and flowers, partly gilt.   16th century.

Lent by DAVID M. CURRIE, ESQ.

529. STEEL KEY chased with arabesque figures and masks, open work and supported by a Corinthian column.   16th century.

Lent by DAVID M. CURRIE, ESQ.

530. PAX, of Silver, partly gilt, chased with the Virgin and Child enthroned, Angels and Saints ; the background minutely ornamented with arabesque designs. 16th century.   Mounted in ebony frame.   From the Hamilton Palace Collection.

Lent by DAVID M. CURRIE, ESQ.

531. STEEL ORNAMENT for a cap.   Representing two Dragons fighting.

Lent by T. FOSTER SHATTOCK, ESQ.

532. STEEL PENDANT embossed with masks, winged female figures, and a medallion portrait of a young lady.   Florentine.   16th century.

Lent by DAVID M. CURRIE, ESQ.

533. Six Crystals, with engravings of the Labours of Hercules. By Valerio Vicentino.
Lent by H. WILLETT, ESQ.

534. Four Crystals, two circular, with helmeted female busts ; two oblong with heads of Bacchus and Faun.
Lent by HENRY WILLETT, ESQ.

535. Case, containing two medals (Pietro Bembo, and Pope Clement VII.), and six coins, (Alexander Sforza, Cosimo de' Medici, and Popes Paul IV. and Clement VII.). By BENVENUTO CELLINI. Lent by MURRAY MARKS, ESQ.

536. Two Heads in wax, illustrating Purgatory and Hell. Two similar heads on a large scale are in the Pitti Palace at Florence. By Zumbo, a Florentine monk.
Lent by J. LUMSDEN PROPERT, ESQ. M.D.

537. Wax Portrait of Eleonora, Duchess of Florence.
Lent by J. LUMSDEN PROPERT, ESQ. M.D.

538. Wax Portraits of Cosimo II. de' Medici and his wife.
Lent by J. LUMSDEN PROPERT, ESQ. M.D.

539. Three Pieces of Enamelled Work, consisting of heads of angels and a group of fruit in brilliant colours. These, with three similar pieces that were in the possession of the late Lady Ruthven, were taken from a gold chalice in the collection of the late Prince Poniatowski, and were said to be the work of Benvenuto Cellini.
Lent by JAMES GURNEY, ESQ.

540. Serving Knife. From the Magniac collection.
Lent by JAMES GURNEY, ESQ.

541. Steel Key of a Cassone, pierced, with monogram surmounted by a coronet.
Lent by JAMES GURNEY, ESQ.

542. Steel Key of a Cassone, of a similar character to the preceding.
Lent by JAMES GURNEY, ESQ.

543. Bronze Medal, with bust of Hercules, *rev.* Hercules receiving the poisoned robe from Lichas. Signed H. B. and a bird.
Lent by JAMES GURNEY, ESQ.

544. BRONZE POMMEL OF A SWORD. Early 15th century.

Lent by R. C. FISHER, ESQ.

545. BRONZE MEDAL OF ENRICO BRUNO, Secretary and Treasurer to Pope Alexander VI., Bishop of Orte and Archbishop of Taranto, d. 1509.

By CARADOSSO.   Lent by R. C. FISHER, ESQ

546. BRONZE MEDAL OF POPE PIUS II.   1458-1464.

By GUAZZALOTTI.   Lent by R. C. FISHER, ESQ.

547. BRONZE MEDAL OF LEO X.   1513-1521.

Lent by R. C. FISHER, ESQ.

548. BRONZE MEDAL, Marco Antonio Magno, son of Celio Magno.   A Venetian.

Lent by R. C. FISHER, ESQ.

549. BRONZE PLAQUE, representing a youth driving a stag towards a satyr.

Lent by R. C. FISHER, ESQ.

550. SILVER MEDAL OF CARDINAL P. BEMBO.

By BENVENUTO CELLINI.   Lent by WILLIAM NEWALL, ESQ.

551. BRONZE MEDAL OF SIGISMONDO PANDOLFO MALATESTA, Lord of Rimini.

Lent by WICKHAM FLOWER, ESQ.

552. BRONZE MEDAL OF ISOTTA DA RIMINI, wife of Sigismondo Pandolfo Malatesta.

Lent by WICKHAM FLOWER, ESQ.

553. BRONZE PLAQUETTE, Judith with head of Holofernes.   From the Spitzer collection.

By RICCIO.   Lent by J. H. FITZHENRY, ESQ.

554. MEDALS with portraits of eight members of the Carrara family.

Lent by J. P. HESELTINE, ESQ.

CASE E.

BRONZES AND PLAQUETTES.

580. BRONZE BUST OF A BOY.   School of Donatello.

Lent by T. G. ARTHUR, ESQ.

581. BRONZE GROUP, Venus and Cupid.

Lent by T. G. ARTHUR, ESQ.

562. BRONZE GROUP, Bacchanal and Satyr.   16th century.

Lent by T. G. ARTHUR, ESQ.

563. BRONZE STATUETTE, Apollo with a lyre.   16th century.

Lent by T. G. ARTHUR, ESQ.

564-5. BRONZE STATUETTES, two Dancing Boys.

Lent by T. G. ARTHUR, ESQ.

566. BRONZE STATUETTE, Crouching Venus; after the antique.   16th century.

Lent by T. G. ARTHUR, ESQ.

567. BRONZE SALT CELLAR, Triton attacked by Serpent.   16th century.

Lent by T. G. ARTHUR, ESQ.

568. BRONZE HEAD OF A BOY.   From the Collection of Baron Denon.   15th century.

Lent by ISAAC FALCKE, ESQ.

569. BRONZE PLAQUETTE, representing the triumph of Eros.   By Andrea Briosco.   15th century.

Lent by ISAAC FALCKE, ESQ.

570. BRONZE INKSTAND, representing the Martyrdom of St. Lawrence.   By Tacca.   16th century.

Lent by MESSRS. DURLACHER BROS.

571. BRONZE FIGURE OF APOLLO, represented somewhat in the attitude of the Apollo Belvedere.   Early 16th century.

Lent by MESSRS. DURLACHER BROS.

572. BRONZE INKSTAND, representing a warrior in antique costume kneeling on his helmet.   The stand and figure are cast in one piece.   North Italian.   Late 15th century.   From the Spitzer collection.

Lent by MESSRS. DURLACHER BROS.

573. PAIR OF BRONZE INCENSE BURNERS, each in the form of a spherical vase surmounted by a Satyr and decorated with masks and garlands.   Late 15th century.   School of Padua.

Lent by MESSRS. DURLACHER BROS.

574. FULL-LENGTH SEATED FEMALE FIGURE, reclining on a backed couch (*cf.* marble statues of Agrippina in the Vatican, Borghese and other Museums).

Lent by JAMES GURNEY, ESQ.

575. BRONZE GROUP, representing Christ at the Pillar. 15th century.
Lent by H. WILLETT, ESQ.

576. BRONZE FIGURE of an old man, bearing the inscription "Ars longa vita brevis."
Lent by H. WILLETT, ESQ.

577. BRONZE INKSTAND. Hercules and Geryon.
Lent by CHARLES BUTLER, ESQ.

578. BRONZE PLAQUETTE, the border composed of thirteen small medallions of Saints ; in the centre the Virgin, and inscription *Regina coeli.* 16th century.
Lent by DAVID M. CURRIE, ESQ.

579. BRONZE PLAQUETTE of a Bacchante ; from a Mirror. By Donatello. 15th century.
Lent by DAVID M. CURRIE, ESQ.

580. BRONZE STATUETTE OF APOLLO, resembling in some respects the Apollo Belvedere. 15th century.
Lent by DAVID M. CURRIE, ESQ.

581. PLAQUETTE. The Virgin and Child. By Antonio Abondio.
Lent by DAVID M. CURRIE, ESQ.

582. BRONZE GROUP. Silenus and Infant Bacchus. 16th Century.
Lent by DAVID M. CURRIE, ESQ.

583. PLAQUE. "Pietà." Richly gilt.
Lent by JAMES GURNEY, ESQ.

584. BRONZE GROUP of the Madonna and Child.
Lent by SIR EDMUND A. H. LECHMERE, BART., M.P.

585. BRONZE PLAQUE. Battle scene.
Lent by the HON. W. F. B. MASSEY-MAINWARING.

586. CIRCULAR BRONZE PLAQUE. The Entry into the Ark.
Lent by the HON. W. F. B. MASSEY-MAINWARING.

587. BRONZE. Figure of the sleeping Hercules.
Lent by J. FLETCHER MOULTON, ESQ., Q.C.

588. BRONZE GROUP. Hercules and Antæus. Florentine.

Lent by WILLIAM NEWALL, ESQ.

589. BRONZE SALT. Man kneeling with shell (for salt) on shoulder.

Lent by WILLIAM NEWALL, ESQ.

590. BRONZE FIGURE OF EROS. By DONATELLO.

Lent by WILLIAM NEWALL, ESQ.

591. BRONZE GOAT.

Lent by the DUKE OF ST. ALBANS.

592. BRONZE HORSE. Attributed to VERROCCHIO.

Lent by C. FAIRFAX-MURRAY, ESQ.

593. BRONZE CANDLESTICK, with figure of a Satyr.

Lent by CHARLES BUTLER, ESQ.

594. BRONZE GILT STATUETTE of Venus crouching.

Lent by the EARL OF WEMYSS.

CASE F.

WOODCARVINGS, &c.

600. CASSONE. Carved in walnut wood.

Lent by SIDNEY ERNEST KENNEDY, ESQ.

601. MARBLE BUST of Warrior in Armour.

Lent by the RT. HON. SIR HENRY AUSTIN LAYARD, G.C.B.

602. MARBLE BUST of the youthful Hercules.

Lent by WILLIAM NEWALL, ESQ.

603. HERCULES reposing ; alabaster. Florentine, 16th century. The figure is painted to resemble bronze ; the background is painted in natural colours.

Lent by J. LUMSDEN PROPERT, ESQ, M.D.

---

604. PAIR OF BELLOWS, carved with a figure of Nature ; bronze gilt nozzle.
Lent by GEORGE DONALDSON, ESQ.

605. ALABASTER PLAQUE, with head and arabesques.
Lent by the HON. W. F. B. MASSEY-MAINWARING.

606. FRAME, carved and gilt, with caryatid figures.
Lent by GEORGE SALTING, ESQ.

607. MARBLE BUST OF INFANT HERCULES. By Tacca.
Lent by the MISSES LOUISA AND LUCY COHEN.

608. PAIR OF CARVED WALNUT WOOD BELLOWS with bronze nozzle, style of Sansovino. 16th century.
Lent by MESSRS. DURLACHER BROS.

609. WAX COMPOSITION, Cupid and Psyche.
Lent by J. LUMSDEN PROPERT, ESQ., M.D.

610. SKETCH OF AN ORNAMENTAL PANEL IN GREEN WAX. Florentine.
Lent by J. LUMSDEN PROPERT, ESQ., M.D.

611. STAMPED LEATHER CASE, of cylindrical form. On the base, figures representing Abundance and Spring. On the cover, four dragons. 16th century.
Lent by FREDERICK DAVIS, ESQ.

612. STAMPED LEATHER CASE, decorated with trophies and a shield of arms. 16th century.
Lent by FREDERICK DAVIS, ESQ.

613. STATUETTE, model for a figure of a fountain. By Giovanni da Bologna.
Lent by the EARL OF WEMYSS.

614. WOODEN BOX, carved. Florentine.
Lent by the BIRMINGHAM MUSEUM AND ART GALLERY.

615. BRONZE PLAQUE. The Virgin and Child. By Donatello.
Lent by J. LUMSDEN PROPERT, ESQ., M.D.

616. REPOUSSÉ SILVER PLAQUE. The Resurrection ; probably the door of a shrine.
Lent by J. LUMSDEN PROPERT, ESQ., M.D.

617. PORTRAIT in wax. Half-length of a General.
Lent by J. LUMSDEN PROPERT, ESQ., M.D.

618. MOSAIC on several tablets, representing the Virgin and the twelve apostles. From the Borghese heirlooms. Roman. 15th century. The large copy from the mosaic is in the Church degli Angeli, in Rome.
Lent by J. LUMSDEN PROPERT, ESQ., M.D.

619. ALABASTER bas relief. The Entombment.
Lent by MRS. VIVIAN.

620. GROUP in boxwood. Hercules and Antæus.
Lent by SAMUEL JOSEPH, ESQ.

621. MARBLE BUST of the youthful St. John the Baptist.
Lent by the EARL OF WEMYSS.

622. CUIR-BOUILLI CASE for knife, fork, and spoon, with the arms of the Della Rovere.
Lent by J. H. FITZHENRY, ESQ.

623. CUIR-BOUILLI CIRCULAR CASE with dome cover.
Lent by J. H. FITZHENRY, ESQ.

CASE G.

PLAQUETTES. LENT BY T. WHITCOMBE GREENE, ESQ.

624. THE VIRGIN AND CHILD, between two candelabre. Surmounted by a palm-leaf with ring for suspension. Pax. Bronze gilt. School of Padua. 15th century.

625. THE VIRGIN AND CHILD. The frame is composed of two pilasters supporting a triangular pediment. Cherubs' heads above. At the base, a coat of arms, and decorated border. The name of the Bishop of Cassano, near Naples, is engraved on the back. MARINVS . TOMACELLVS . EPS . CASSAN. Pax. Bronze gilt. End of 15th century.

626. THE ENTRY OF CHRIST INTO JERUSALEM. Bronze, cast from a Byzantine ivory.

627. THE VIRGIN AND CHILD. Bronze, enamelled, with rich border of leaves, flowers and fruit. MP . ΘY inscribed over the head of the Virgin, and corresponding letters over the Infant Saviour. Cast from a Byzantine ivory of the 13th century

628. THE DEAD CHRIST, attended by the three Marys and four other figures. Landscape in the background. Above, groups of angels. Bronze gilt. 15th century

629. THE MARTYRDOM OF ST. JOHN. Bronze, parcel gilt. 16th century.

630. THE HOLY FAMILY. On the left an angel presenting a youth. Bronze. 16th century.

631. THE DEAD CHRIST, attended by the two Marys. Bronze gilt. 15th century.

632: CHRIST HEALING THE LEPERS. Bronze ; oval. 16th century.

633. THE DEAD CHRIST, surrounded by St. Joseph, the two Marys, and two other figures. Bronze gilt. 15th century.

634. ST. JEROME, kneeling before a crucifix. Pax. Bronze gilt. 16th century.

635. ST. JOHN THE BAPTIST. Pax. Bronze. 16th century.

636. THE ANNUNCIATION. Bronze. 16th century.

637. AN ANGEL bearing a lily. Bronze. 16th century.

638 FEMALE FIGURE emblematic of Learning, holding a book in right hand, and in left a torch, which is illumined by two angels. Bronze gilt. 16th century.

639. FIGURE OF AN ARCHER discharging an arrow. Bronze. School of Donatello. 15th century.

640. AMORINI playing with a mask. Bronze. School of Donatello. 15th century.

641. AUGUSTUS (as Mercury) and Abundantia. Bronze. By Cristoforo di Geremia. 1450–1468. ·

642. ST. JEROME. Bronze. By Ulocrino. End of 15th century.

643. APOLLO AND MARSYAS. Bronze. By Ulocrino.

644. THE DEATH OF MELEAGER. Meleager, seated on a rock, is leaning back, apparently at the point of death ; at his feet lies the head of the Calydonian boar. Standing at a burning altar, and holding out a horned mask towards her son, Althæa throws the fatal brand into the flames. Bronze By Ulocrino.

645. APOLLO AND MARSYAS. Olympus intercedes for his master. Bronze, after the antique. 15th century.

646. HERCULES AND THE NEMÆAN LION. Bronze. 15th century.

647. BOY PLAYING A FLAGEOLET. Side of a salt-cellar. Bronze. 15th century.

648. DIOMED AND THE PALLADIUM. After the antique. Bronze. 15th centur ·.

649. THE FALL OF PHAETON. A landscape in the background. Bronze. End of 15th century.

650. VULCAN FORGING THE ARMS OF ÆNEAS. In the centre Victory, winged, gives a buckler to Æneas ; in the foreground, two horses drinking. Bronze. School of Padua. 15th century.

651. VULCAN FORGING THE WINGS OF CUPID. Bronze. North Italian. End of 15th century.

652. VULCAN FORGING ARROWS FOR CUPID. Legend, AMOR VINCIT OMNIA. Bronze. North Italian. End of 15th century. Probably after an antique gem.

653. ORPHEUS CHARMING THE ANIMALS. End of 15th century.

654. SATYR. As represented in the famous Martelli mirror-case, attributed to Donatello. Bronze.

655. BACCHANTE. The corresponding figure in the same group. Iron repoussé.

656. COMBAT between horseman and foot-soldier, both armed with spears; the figures nude. Bronze. 15th century. By Melioli, of Mantua, 1474—1488.

657. SEAL OF LORENZO ROVERELLA, Bishop of Ferrara 1460—1474. Under a triple canopy, St. George is attacking the Dragon. On the left appears the daughter of the King of Lydia. In the lower compartment the bishop is kneeling with crozier and mitre. An escutcheon on either side. Legend in Gothic capitals. Bronze.

658. A TRITON carrying a Nereid through the waves; beside them floats an Amorino. 15th century.

659. THE JUSTICE OF TRAJAN. Bronze. 15th century.

660. HUNTING PARTY IN A WOOD. Bronze. 15th century.

661. APOLLO, in quadriga. Bronze. 15th century.

662. ROMAN SOLDIERS putting out the eyes of prisoners. Bronze. 15th century.

663. COMBAT OF WARRIORS, on horse and foot. Bronze. 16th century.

664. NESSUS AND DEJANEIRA. Bronze. 15th century.

665. A YOUTH, supporting a large scroll, lies wounded by a dart from Cupid standing on a tree, from the branches of which fragments of human limbs are hanging. Cupid in turn is attacked by Minerva descending through the air with sword and shield. A female figure approaches with gestures of grief. Bronze. Probably by the artist who signs LCRIIS, and L. I. C. 15th century. Unpublished.

666. GROUP OF ROMAN FIGURES, five in an upper compartment and five in a lower. Engraved at the back ANTONINO PIO PALESTRINA. Bronze.

667. HELEN OF TROY. A fantastic composition. On the reverse, Paris. Bronze 15th century.

668. AUGUSTUS CÆSAR. Medallion in foliated border and square frame. One of the sides of an inkstand. Bronze. 15th century.

669. APOLLO AND DAPHNE. Bronze gilt. 16th century.

670. CUPID asleep, his right arm resting on an altar, on which his bow and quiver are suspended. By Fra Antonio da Brescia Early 16th century.

671. A BACCHANTE sleeping, with two children behind her, near a pillar on which is written VIRTUS. Two Satyrs approach from the right. By Fra Antonio da Brescia.

WORKS OF GIOVANNI DI LORENZO DI PIETRO DELLE OPERE, CALLED GIOVANNI DELLE CORNIOLE OF FLORENCE. 1470-1516.

672. ARIADNE in the Isle of Naxos. Ariadne seated in the midst of a Bacchanalian group, holds a large torch turned to the ground. The surrounding figures bear aloft various emblems, or spoils of the chase, such as the heads of a bull, a boar, and a lion. To the left a Satyr carries on his shoulders a female faun. Signed "IO, F. F." Bronze, the figures gilt : convex.

673. THE JUDGMENT OF PARIS. Bronze.

674. MUCIUS SCÆVOLA. Scævola attended by a group of horsemen, standard-bearers, and others, standing before an altar, thrusts his right hand into the flames. Bronze. Escutcheon-shaped.

675. THE FABLE OF THE BUNDLE OF STICKS. Bronze. Escutcheon-shaped.

676. ALLEGORICAL SUBJECT. On the right appears a woman seated on a dragon, attended by another behind her ; she is approached by a youth holding a palm-branch, while another bears a human head ; on the left a statue of Artemis, and a bear (her symbol). Bronze.

677. A BULL AND A LION. On a tablet above, suspended by ribbons, is inscribed CONSTANTIA. Bronze. Artist unknown. *Cir.* 1500.

678. PEGASUS attended by three of the Muses. Bronze. 16th century.

G 2

679. DAPHNE, clad in a long flowing robe flees before Apollo : her arms are already transformed into laurels. Architectural background. Bronze. End of 15th century.

680. AN ANCIENT SACRIFICE. Minute work of many figures contained within a shield. Signed OP. VICTORIS. CAMELL. V. By Vittore Gambello, called Camelio, of Venice. 1455-1537. Bronze gilt, square. Unpublished.

681. DIOMED AND THE PALLADIUM. Bronze. Oval. 15th century.

WORKS OF MODERNO, AN ARTIST OF NORTHERN ITALY.
END OF THE FIFTEENTH CENTURY TO 1530.

682. DAVID AND GOLIATH. Bronze. Circular.

683. THE VIRGIN AND CHILD. An Angel on either side. Bronze gilt.

684. THE ADORATION OF THE MAGI. Bronze.

685. THE PRESENTATION IN THE TEMPLE. Bronze.

686. THE FLAGELLATION. Bronze.

687. THE CRUCIFIXION. Bronze.

688. THE ENTOMBMENT. Bronze.

689. THE ENTOMBMENT ; another composition, in the style of Mantegna. Bronze gilt.

690. THE RESURRECTION. Bronze.

691. AUGUSTUS AND THE SIBYL. Bronze gilt.

692. MARS AND VICTORY. Bronze.

693. THE FALL OF PHAETON. Bronze.

694. HERCULES AND CACUS. Bronze. Square. A reduction of the usual size.

695. HERCULES STRANGLING THE MONSTER GERYON. Bronze.

696. HERCULES AND THE NEMÆAN LION. Bronze gilt. Circular.

697. HERCULES CLEARING THE AUGEAN STABLES. Bronze.

698. ORPHEUS AND EURYDICE. Orpheus plays a violin before Pluto, represented as a winged demon ; near him stands Eurydice. In the background, two demons. Bronze.

699. LUCRETIA. Bronze.

700. A LION HUNT. Bronze.

701. FEMALE FIGURE playing a Lute, moving rapidly forward to the right. Bronze.

702. HERCULES AND THE NEMÆAN LION. In the small medallion above, the Judgment of Solomon ; in the lower, Hercules and Achelous. Bronze, the ends arched.

703. HERCULES AND ANTÆUS. Bronze.

WORKS OF ANDREA BRIOSCO, CALLED IL RICCIO, OF PADUA.
1470–1532.

704. NESSUS AND DEIANEIRA. The Centaur galloping through the river. Bronze, in high relief.

705. AN ANCIENT SACRIFICE. A group of numerous figures with architectural background. Bronze.

706. A WOMAN RECLINING, asleep, against a vase, holds in her right hand an open book, which two Amorini are reading. In the exergue : ΣΕΜΝΗΚΛΟΠΙΑ. Bronze.

707. ALLEGORICAL SUBJECT   A genius trampling on a Satyr; with his left hand he pulls down a tree, to which wings are attached. With his right he pours out the contents of a vase. On the right is seen an emblem of the wind. A chastening of Calumny. Bronze. Circular.

708. THE DEATH OF DIDO. She pierces her breast with a dagger. Near her burns a funeral pile. Landscape in the background. At the foot of a tree on the left is the signature " A. R." Bronze, in high relief.

WORKS OF VALERIO BELLI, CALLED VICENTINO. 1465-1546.
PLAQUETTES CAST FROM ENGRAVINGS ON ROCK CRYSTAL.

709. THE ADORATION OF THE SHEPHERDS. Bronze. Oval.

710. THE ADORATION OF THE MAGI.   On the reverse, The Presentation in the Temple. Bronze. Rectangular.

711. THE KISS OF JUDAS. Bronze. Oval.

712. THE ENTOMBMENT. Bronze.

713. THE ENTOMBMENT. Bronze. Cval.

714. THE ENTOMBMENT. Bronze gilt. Oval.

715. CHRIST BEARING THE CROSS. Bronze. Oval.

716. A LION HUNT. Bronze. Oval.

717. THE TRIUMPH OF AMPHITRITE.   The Goddess drawn by sea-horses through the waves, attended by Tritons and Nereids. Bronze. Oval.

WORKS OF GIOVANNI BERNARDI DA CASTEL BOLOGNESE. CAST FROM ENGRAVINGS ON ROCK CRYSTAL. 1496-1553.

718. THE MEETING OF ELEAZAR AND REBECCA. Bronze ; oval.

719. VENUS AND DIANA. Victory flying above bestows on the one a crown, on the other an arrow. Bronze ; oval.

720. PROMETHEUS AND THE VULTURE. Bronze ; oval.

721. THE RAPE OF THE SABINES. Bronze ; oval.

722. THE HORATII AND CURIATII. Bronze ; oval.

723. COMBAT OF CAVALRY. On the left a river god reclining on his urn. A spirited group of many figures. Bronze gilt ; oval.

724. A BOAR HUNT. A group of six figures around the boar, one of whom bears a shield ornamented with six lilies. Bronze ; oval. Unpublished.

725. THE FALL OF PHAETON. Above, Phaeton cast headlong ; below, Eridanus and three Nymphs transformed into poplars. Bronze ; oval. A composition said to have been engraved from a design by Michelangelo.

---

726. BACCHUS AND CERES, in a frame richly ornamented with amorini, fruit and flowers. Bronze. 16th century.

727. CUPID FORGING CHAINS. Bronze ; oval. 16th century.

728. SCIPIO AFRICANUS. Bronze ; oval. From an antique gem. 15th century.

729. CENTAUR. Bronze ; oval.

730. A SERIES OF TWELVE SMALL PLAQUETTES. (Diana, Esculapius, Pan, &c.) After the antique. Bronze.

731. BACCHANALIAN GROUP. Bronze ; oval. From a gem.

732. MARCUS CURTIUS. Bronze gilt. In frame decorated with satyrs, &c. Plaquette for the hat. 15th century.

733. LAOCOON. Bronze gilt. In border. Hat plaquette. 15th century.

734. FEMALE BUST. With border. Bronze. Hat plaquette. 16th century.

735. FAUSTINA. Bronze. Hat plaquette. 16th century.

736. LUCRETIA. Bronze gilt ; small oval.

737. FRANCIS I. OF FRANCE. Bronze gilt. Hat plaquette.

738. CHARLES V., EMPEROR OF GERMANY. Bronze gilt. Hat plaquette. *Circa* 1520.

739. CHARLES V., with border. Bronze gilt. Hat plaquette. *Circa* 1540.

740. ST. GEORGE AND THE DRAGON. Gilt bronze, with ornamental border. A mounting attached to hold a plume. For a horse's bit. 16th century.

741. EUROPA AND THE BULL. Gilt bronze with ornamental border. 16th century

742. WARRIOR IN QUADRIGA. Gilt bronze. 16th century.

743. COMBAT OF HORSEMEN. Gilt bronze. Convex, companion to 742.

744. FEMALE HEAD, encircled with vine leaves and grapes, within a border partly enamelled. Bronze. Used for a horse's bit. 16th century.

745. MORSE, engraved with the figure of a bishop. Bronze gilt. 14th century.

746. MIRROR-CASE. Repoussé silver gilt with traces of enamel. Venus, accompanied by Cupid, is crowned by Victory, who also gives an arrow to Diana. A composition by G. Bernardi (see No. 719).

747. THE ADORATION OF THE MAGI. Niello on silver. Shield with arms of the Visconti. 16th century.

748. THE ADORATION OF THE SHEPHERDS. Silver plaque minutely engraved 16th century.

749. TERRA COTTA FIGURE OF ATLAS, painted in natural colours. Ascribed to Giovanni da Bologna and said to have been made for one of the Medici.
Lent by F. A. WHITE, ESQ.

750. TERRA COTTA BUST OF A GIRL.
Lent by LORD BATTERSEA.

751. PHARMACY JAR of Majolica, with shield of arms in front.
Lent by FREDERICK DAVIS, ESQ.

752. MARBLE BUST OF A GIRL.
Lent by the EARL OF WEMYSS.

753. FOUNTAIN. Figure of youth, one foot on dolphin, holding shell. School of Michelangelo. Florentine ; early 16th century.
Lent by H. PFUNGST, ESQ.

754. BRONZE FIGURE OF HERCULES, signed "Baccio Bandinelli Fio antico 1556." From the Hamilton Palace Collection.
"Baccio excelled in making bronze figures a braccia high, from antique models."— *Vasari.*
Lent by JAMES GURNEY, ESQ.

755. CARVING IN WOOD of a boy in the character of Hercules.
Lent by the RIGHT HON. SIR HENRY AUSTIN LAYARD, G C.B.

756. PIETÀ in terra-cotta.
Lent by the EARL OF WEMYSS.

757. MAJOLICA VASE with two handles. Subject from the Metamorphoses of Ovid.
Lent by the DUKE OF ST. ALBANS.

758. TERRA COTTA BUST OF CHRIST, painted in natural colours.
Lent by LORD BATTERSEA.

759. CAFFAGIOLO VASE. The Judgment of Paris.
Lent by CHARLES BUTLER, ESQ.

760. BRONZE BUST OF A GIRL. By Donatello.
Lent by the DUKE OF WESTMINSTER.

761. BRONZE FIGURE OF DAVID. He holds in his right hand a stone. By Michelangelo.
Lent by GEORGE SALTING, ESQ.

NORTH GALLERY.

CASE H.

IVORIES

762. IVORY CRUCIFIX. A picture painted on the stand, probably by Annibale Caracci.
Lent by the RECTOR OF STONYHURST COLLEGE.

763. IVORY STATUETTE. The Flagellation.
Lent by MRS. P. C. HARDWICK.

764. IVORY STATUETTE. The Flagellation.
Lent by WICKHAM FLOWER, ESQ.

765. IVORY CARVING OF EIGHT PANELS, with figures of St. Augustine, St. Antony of Padua, and romance subjects.
Lent by CHARLES BUTLER, ESQ.

766. TRIPTYCH IN IVORY, with scenes from the life of Christ.
Lent by the RIGHT REV. THE BISHOP OF PORTSMOUTH.

767. TRIPTYCH IN IVORY, representing the Madonna and Child with Saints.
Lent by CHARLES BUTLER, ESQ.

768. IVORY GROUP OF THE VIRGIN AND CHILD. Signed "Bianchi," dated 1507.
Lent by MRS. P. C. HARDWICK.

769. IVORY CASKET, with figures of Jongleurs. Early 14th century.
Lent by MRS. P. C. HARDWICK.

770. INLAID IVORY AND EBONY BOX, arranged for chess and backgammon.
Lent by CHARLES BUTLER, ESQ.

771. INLAID CASKET OF TARSIA WORK.

Lent by CHARLES BUTLER, ESQ.

772 CARVED AND INLAID IVORY CASKET, with figures.

Lent by CHARLES BUTLER, ESQ.

773. PAIR OF IVORY STATUETTES. One of Venus with Cupid ; the other, Paris, holding the apple in his hand.

Lent by ALFRED DE ROTHSCHILD, ESQ.

774. IVORY PLAQUE, part of casket or book cover. 12th century.

Lent by MRS. P. C. HARDWICK.

775. IVORY CASKET. Florentine. 15th century

Lent by J. LUMSDEN PROPERT, ESQ., M.D.

776. EBONY WRITING-DESK, delicately inlaid with ivory ; subjects from the Old Testament and the Twelve Months.

Lent by FREDERICK DAVIS, ESQ.

777. OCTAGONAL CASKET, inlaid with tortoiseshell and ivory plaques, carved in relief. Malatesta arms and the initials of Isotta da Rimini are carved on one side of the plaques. Said to be a gift to Isotta from her husband, Sigismondo Pandolfo Malatesta, Lord of Rimini, about 1460.

Lent by J. H. MIDDLETON, ESQ., LL.D.

778. TABERNACLE. Christ in ivory, on silver stand.

Lent by CHARLES BUTLER, ESQ.

779. BONE HAND REST FOR A SCRIBE, terminating in carved figure.

Lent by CHARLES BUTLER, ESQ.

780. IVORY NEEDLE-CASE, engraved with battle scene. Signed " Bartolomeo Sforza faciebat, 1584."

Lent by JAMES GURNEY, ESQ.

781. CARVED IVORY EWER. Vine leaves terminating in masks.

Lent by ALFRED DE PASS, ESQ.

782. IVORY FLORENTINE CASKET.

Lent by LADY TREVELYAN

783. A PASTORAL STAFF in carved bone—14th century.

The head of this crosier is composed as follows :—The knob is a large rhomboidal mass, formed from a square block by cutting off the angles so as to leave four lozenge-shaped spaces at the sides ; these are filled in with emblems of the Evangelists carved in low relief. The shaft of the volute rises above this in the shape of a dragon's head and neck, with gaping mouth, from which grows the volute, enriched on the outer margin with ten boldly projecting leaf-shaped crockets rudely carved ; the volute encloses the lamb with the stem of a cross or banner, the upper part of which is broken away ; also in the upper part is a dove. The extremity of the volute forms another dragon's head, with gaping mouth thickly set with teeth, and apparently menacing the lamb ; the head and shaft of the crosier are diapered over with floral ornaments, rosettes, grotesque dragons, and other animals, rather coarsely executed in surface gilding, outlined with red and black. Other crosiers of this identical type, most likely produced in the same district and at the same period, are still preserved ; they are apparently of north Italian origin. It is difficult to determine their approximate date with any certainty ; it is probably, however, later than might be at first supposed. The quasi-Byzantine style, especially marked in the diapered ornaments painted on them, would apparently indicate the 13th or earlier part of the 14th century ; but, judging from other details of a more modern aspect, it seems more likely that these seemingly very ancient motives were only traditionally retained in some remote districts.

Crosiers enclosing a lamb, with a cross in the volute, menaced by a dragon, were a favourite type, particularly in the 12th, 13th, and 14th centuries. As a mystical emblem of the contest of our Saviour with the evil one, this design is too obvious to require further elucidation.

MESSRS. J. DUVEEN & SON.

784. IVORY STATUETTE OF A HUNTRESS on marble pedestal, part of an allegory of "Vanities," designed by Mantegna. From the Cathedral at Volaterra.

Lent by J. LUMSDEN PROPERT, ESQ., M.D.

785. IVORY FIGURE of the infant St. John.

Lent by PHILIP F. WALKER, ESQ.

786. BONE HAND REST FOR A SCRIBE.

Lent by CHARLES BUTLER, ESQ.

787. IVORY BOX. Oval. Neptune and Amphitrite.

Lent by MRS. P. C. HARDWICK.

788. IVORY FIGURE OF A CENTAUR.

Lent by PHILIP F. WALKER, ESQ.

789. IVORY STATUETTE. Prometheus. 13th century.

Lent by MRS. P. C. HARDWICK.

790. BONE PLAQUE, an Angel leaning on a column.

Lent by MRS. BLOOD.

791. BONE PLAQUE, a winged figure holding a globe.

Lent by MRS. BLOOD.

792. IVORY DEVOTIONAL MEDALLION, carved both sides and signed.

Lent by ALFRED DE PASS, ESQ.

793. IVORY DEVOTIONAL PENDANT, with figures of St. Francis and St. Antony of Padua.

Lent by ALFRED DE PASS, ESQ.

794. CARVING IN IVORY ; medallion with bust of Pope Sixtus V. on a pedestal, on which Christ is giving the keys to St. Peter. By Fiammingo.

Lent by WILLIAM BOORE, ESQ.

795. AN IVORY CARVING. Two boys at play.

Lent by JAMES GURNEY, ESQ.

796. BONE PANELS. Three female figures.

Lent by MRS. BLOOD.

797. INLAID BONE CASKET, carved with figures.

Lent by CHARLES BUTLER, ESQ.

798. HANDLE FOR A FEATHER FAN in carved ivory, designed by Lelio Orsi. Early 16th Century.

Lent by MESSRS. DURLACHER BROS.

799. IVORY PLAQUE, representing Vulcan, Venus, and Cupid.

Lent by MRS. P. C. HARDWICK.

800. PAIR OF CARVED ALABASTER BRACKETS, gilt.

Lent by ALFRED DE PASS, ESQ.

801. A MEDICINE CHEST, containing a secret drawer for antidotes to poisons, formerly belonging to COSIMO DE' MEDICI.

Lent by HENRY WILLETT, ESQ.

802. IVORY BUST OF COSIMO DE' MEDICI. By Alguardi.

Lent by HENRY WILLETT, ESQ.

803. KNIFE, FORK AND SPOON, with carved ivory handles.

Lent by CHARLES BUTLER, ESQ.

804. CARVED IVORY NEEDLE-CASE.

Lent by MRS. BLOOD.

805. A LION, in ivory. 16th century

Lent by ISAAC FALCKE, ESQ.

806. IVORY PANEL, with a man and woman.

Lent by MRS. COWELL.

807. IVORY PLAQUE, representing David with head of Goliath.

Lent by MRS. P. C. HARDWICK.

CASE I.

MAJOLICA.

MAJOLICA. LENT BY GEORGE SALTING, ESQ.

815. DRUG POT, enamelled earthenware, painted with an armed horseman and floral bands. Faenza. 16th century.

816. PLATE, enamelled earthenware, painted with portrait of a lady and name "Proserphina." Castel-Durante. 16th century.

817. DISH, majolica, painted with trophies, &c., on blue ground. Faenza. 16th century.

818. PLATE, majolica, with male bust of "Ramazotta." Faenza. 16th century.

819. VASE, majolica, two-handled, painted with armorial shields and floral ornaments on orange ground. Faenza. 16th century.

820. EWER, enamelled earthenware, painted with a shield of arms, scrolls, and gadroons in polychrome. Faenza or Pesaro. 16th century.

821. PLATE, enamelled earthenware, majolica, painted and lustred with a portrait of a lady in the centre surrounded by imbrications ; border of floral design. Gubbio. 16th century.

822. PLATEAU, earthenware, painted in colours with the Triumph of the Church over infidels and heretics. Attributed to Orazio Fontana. Urbino. Dated 1543.

823. PLATE, majolica, painted with a group of four named persons within a building. Urbino. 16th century.

824. PLATE, majolica, painted with figure of Cupid, masks, and scroll-work.   Urbino. 16th century.

825. DISH, majolica, painted with the Rape of Helen.   Urbino.   16th century.

826. PLATE, lustred majolica, painted with military trophies and arabesques.   Gubbio. Dated 1530.

827. EWER, majolica, painted with the Baptism of Christ.   Urbino.   16th century.

828. DRUG POT, enamelled earthenware, painted in polychrome with a captive brought before a king in a tent.   Urbino.   16th century.

829. DISH, lustred majolica, painted with a bust of a lady and floral scrolls.   Pesaro. 16th century.

830. PLATE, majolica, sunk centre, painted with the story of Psyche.   Urbino.   16th century.

831. DISH, majolica, painted with a shield surrounded by borders of blue ornament. Caffaggiolo.   16th century.

832. PLATE, glazed earthenware, in the centre a medallion enclosing a sleeping animal, round the border are two shields and two labels with music amid arabesques on blue.   Mark of the Casa Pirota fabrique.   Faenza.   16th century.

833. PLATE, enamelled earthenware, painted with heraldic shields, scroll foliage and cornucopia.   Faenza.   First half of 16th century.

834. PLATE, lustred majolica, painted by Maestro Giorgio with a heraldic shield surrounded by a foliated border on blue ground.   Gubbio.   Dated 1527.

835. PLATE, enamelled earthenware, majolica, painted and lustred with a shield of arms in the centre surrounded by a border of four medallions, separated by grotesques. Gubbio.   16th century.

836. DISH, majolica, with grotesques and busts.   Faenza.   Dated 1526.

837. DISH, majolica, with bust of Cæsar.   Siena.

CASE J.

BRONZES AND MEDALS.

838. TERRA COTTA FIGURE OF CHARITY.

Lent by the EARL OF WEMYSS.

839. BRONZE MODEL OF A FOUNTAIN. Attributed to Giovanni da Bologna. 16th century.

Lent by ISAAC FALCKE, ESQ.

840. BRONZE STATUETTE. Victory. Florentine. 16th century.

Lent by T. WHITCOMBE GREENE, ESQ.

841. HAND-BELL. Richly decorated with foliage ornaments in sharp relief. The central zone is adorned with figures of the Virgin, Saints, and the bust of a Pope. Bell-metal. 16th century.

Lent by T. WHITCOMBE GREENE, ESQ.

842. HANDLE, formed as the double-head of a lion. Bronze. 15th century.

Lent by T. WHITCOMBE GREENE, ESQ.

843. EMBLEMATICAL FIGURE OF TIME, represented as a young child in recumbent posture, holding a human skull; his left arm rests on an hour-glass. The base bears the following inscription:—IL. TEMPO. PASSA. E. LA. MORTO. VIEN. PRIO. . . A. CHI. NON. FA. BEN. FAC. MALO. MA. ESPERAMO. I. BE. IL. TEMPO. PASSA. FIRMO. Bronze. 15th century.

Lent by T. WHITCOMBE GREENE, ESQ.

844. HAND-BELL. Decorated with arabesque ornamentation and armorial escutcheons, supported by hippocamps. On one shield a portrait is represented ; on another the cross of the Knights of Malta. A small medallion bears the signature of the maker : IOSEPH . DE . LEVIS . VER . F. Bell-metal. 16th century.

The same artist's name appears on the large pair of fire-dogs, now in the South Kensington Museum, made for the Venetian family of Barberigo. "Josepho . di . Levi . in . Verona . me . fece."

Lent by T. WHITCOMBE GREENE, ESQ.

845. BRONZE INKSTAND. By Riccio.

Lent by J. H. FITZHENRY, ESQ.

845*. FIGURE OF ST. SEBASTIAN. Lead.

Lent by P. F. WALKER, ESQ.

846. CANDLESTICK. The triangular base is formed of three half-figures of winged boys, terminating in foliage and strap-work. The upper part is decorated with a corresponding design, the figures being connected by garlands of flowers Bronze. 16th Century.

Lent by T. WHITCOMBE GREENE, ESQ.

847. STATUETTE. Athlete holding a disc. Bronze. Early 16th Century.

Lent by T. WHITCOMBE GREENE, ESQ.

848. LAMP. Decorated with masks, strap-work and acanthus foliage, the handle formed by two snakes intertwined. Bronze. 15th Century.

Lent by T. WHITCOMBE GREENE, ESQ.

849. BOY seated on a pillar, his right hand resting on a dolphin. At the base, heads of sea-monsters. Bronze. 16th Century.

Lent by T. WHITCOMBE GREENE, ESQ.

850. STATUETTE. Female figure holding a circular tray. Bronze. 16th Century.

Lent by T. WHITCOMBE GREENE, ESQ.

851. LAOCOON AND HIS SONS destroyed by serpents. A variation of the antique composition. Bronze. 15th Century.

Lent by T. WHITCOMBE GREENE, ESQ.

852. A DRAGON, posed on its back, with outstretched wings. Bronze. 15th Century.

Lent by T. WHITCOMBE GREENE, ESQ.

853. BRONZE KNOCKER.

Lent by the EARL OF WEMYSS.

854. BRONZE CUP.

Lent by the EARL OF WEMYSS.

855. BRONZE FIGURE OF GLADIATOR.

Lent by J. FLETCHER MOULTON, ESQ., Q.C.

856. BRONZE CANDLESTICK. The base decorated with masks.

Lent by the EARL OF WEMYSS.

857. BRONZE MORTAR. Round the rim, in raised letters, "Bartolomeo Daverazzaon. MCCCCXX."

Lent by JAMES GURNEY, ESQ.

H

858. BRONZE PITCHER.

Lent by the EARL OF WEMYSS.

859. BRONZE INKSTAND.   Two bacchanalian figures supporting stand.   One of the figures also holds nozzle for candle.

Lent by the EARL OF WEMYSS.

860. ATLAS SUPPORTING THE GLOBE.   On a triangular base decorated with foliage, standing on lions' feet.   At one of the corners is a shell for ink.   The sphere, which opens into two parts, forms a lamp.   The upper half is adorned with representations of the sun and stars, and is surmounted by the figure of a young child.   Attributed to Andrea Riccio, of Padua.   Bronze.   15th Century.

Lent by T. WHITCOMBE GREENE, ESQ.

861. LAMP.   In the shape of a grotesque dragon; the tail, curled over the back, forming the handle.   The lower jaw holds the burner.   Beneath is inscribed, NE. QUIS. ALIVD.   Bronze.   15th Century.

Lent by T. WHITCOMBE GREENE, ESQ.

862. LION, seated.   Bronze.   15th Century.

Lent by T. WHITCOMBE GREENE, ESQ.

863. STATUETTE.   Lucretia.   Bronze.   Early 16th Century.

Lent by T. WHITCOMBE GREENE, ESQ.

864. BRONZE DOOR HANDLE AND MASK, the former formed of mermaids.

Lent by CHARLES BUTLER, ESQ.

865. FEMALE terminal figure holding a cup in the left hand.   Bronze: parcel-gilt.   Early 16th Century.

Lent by T. WHITCOMBE GREENE, ESQ.

866. BRONZE DOOR HANDLE AND MASK, the former formed of mermaids.

Lent by CHARLES BUTLER, ESQ.

867. BRONZE INKSTAND.   15th Century.

Lent by CHARLES BUTLER, ESQ.

868. LAMP.   A sandalled foot.   Bronze.   15th Century.

Lent by T. WHITCOMBE GREENE, ESQ.

869. STATUETTE. Apollo, holding a lyre. Bronze. 16th Century.

Lent by T. WHITCOMBE GREENE, ESQ.

870. LAMP. A grotesque horned female sphinx, decorated with strap-work and acanthus foliage. A snail forms the nozzle. Bronze. 15th or early 16th Century.

Lent by T. WHITCOMBE GREENE, ESQ.

MEDALS AND COINS. LENT BY J. P. HESELTINE, ESQ.

871. FILIPPO MARIA VISCONTI, Duke of Milan, 1412-1447, silver. By Pisano.

872. ALFONSO V., King of Aragon, 1442-1458. By Pisano.

873. NICCOLO PICCININI, Condottiere, 1380-1444. By Pisano.

874. LEONELLO D'ESTE, 1441-1450. By Pisano.

875. FEDERIGO DE MONTEFELTRO, Duke of Urbino, 1443-1482. By Sperandio.

876. JACOPO TROTTI, of Ferrara, Secretary of Borso d'Este. By Sperandio.

877. MICHAEL ANGELO BUONAROTTI, Painter and Sculptor, 1475-1564. By Leone Leoni.

878. GIOVANNI MOCENIGO, Doge of Venice, 1478-1485. By G. J. F.

879. LUCRETIA BORGIA, 1480-1519.

880. GENTILE BELLINI, painter, 1426-1507. By Camelio.

881. GIULIA ASTALIA. By Talpa.

882. MADDELINA, a lady of Mantua. By Pomedello.

883. JACOBA CORRIGIA. By Pomedello.

884. UNKNOWN PORTRAIT. By Caroto?

885. CHARLES V., Emperor.

H 2

886. NICHOLAS V., Pope, 1447-1455. By Guazzalotti.

887. PAOLO GIOVIO, Bishop of Nocera, 1528-1552. By Sangallo.

888. FRANCESCO DE SANGALLO, sculptor, 1494-1676. By himself.

889. PAUL III., Pope, 1534-1550. By Valerio Belli.

890. SEBASTIANO RENIERI   A Venetian.

891. ELISABETTA QUIRINI.

892. UNKNOWN FEMALE PORTRAIT.

893. LUCRETIA DE' MEDICI, wife of Alfonso II. d'Este. By Pastorino of Siena.

894. NICOLO PUZZOLO.

895. BATTISTA SPANIOLI, Theologian and Poet, 1448-1516.

896. LEONARDO ZANTANI, unknown.

897. MARCO CROTO, 1500-1525.

898. ROBERTO BRICCONET, Archbishop of Rheims and Chancellor of France, 1493-1497.

899. PORTRAIT OF TINTORETTO.

900. ALBERTO BELLI, jurist of Perugia. By Niccolo Fiorentino.

901. BINDO ALTOVITI, of Florence, 1490-1556. By Benvenuto Cellini.

902. PAUL III. Pope, 1534-1550. By Valerio Belli.

903. FIGURE OF CUPID. Reverse, Apollo and Dragon.

904-5. GIANGALEAZZO MARIA SFORZA, Duke of Milan, 1476-1494, gold ducat and silver testoon, ascribed to Lionardo da Vinci.

CASE K.

MUSICAL INSTRUMENTS.

906. SPINET OF PENTAGONAL FORM. Case covered in ruby velvet. The name board painted with classical subjects, surrounded by arabesque borders upon mother-of-pearl. In the right-hand panel Apollo and Marsyas playing upon the viol and syrinx. The compass represents four octaves. Signed " Joannes Celestini, MDXCIII."
> Lent by G. DONALDSON, ESQ.

907. CETERA. The head carved with two figures of Satyrs surmounted by a female head. This interesting instrument is said to have belonged to Titian, and was formerly in the collection of the singer Mario at Florence. It became subsequently the property of Rossini, the composer, at whose death it was purchased by the exhibitor. Signed " Gironimo Campi." Brescian. 15th Century.
> Lent by G. DONALDSON, ESQ.

908. CETERA. Richly covered with figures and scrolls in low relief. Formerly in the Biblioteca Estense at Modena. North Italian. 1520.
> Lent by G. DONALDSON, ESQ.

909. REBEC.
> Lent by G. DONALDSON, ESQ.

CASE L.

MEDALS. LENT BY T. WHITCOMBE GREENE, ESQ.

ITALIAN PORTRAIT MEDALS.

910. MALATESTA NOVELLO, Lord of Cesena. 1418-1465. By Vittore Pisano.

911. ALFONSO V., of Aragon, King of Sicily and Naples. 1394-1458. Reverse (shown). An eagle abandoning his prey to vultures. By Vittore Pisano.

912. The same. Plaquette. By Vittore Pisano.

913. PALEOLOGOS (Joannes VII.), Emperor of the East, 1390-1448. Lead. By Vittore Pisano.

914. VITTORINO DA FELTRE. Scholar, 1379-1447. By Vittore Pisano.

915. NICCOLO III. D'ESTE, Lord of Ferrara, 1384-1441. Lead. Attributed to Vittore Pisano.

916. SIGISMONDO PANDOLFO MALATESTA, Lord of Rimini, 1417-1468. By Matteo di Pasti.

917. ISOTTA DA RIMINI, wife of S. P. Malatesta. The head covered with a veil. By Matteo di Pasti.

918. The same, with head uncovered. By Matteo di Pasti.

919. BENEDETTO DI PASTI, brother of the Artist. Lead. By Matteo di Pasti.

920. GIOVANNI TAVELLI, of Tossignano, Bishop of Ferrara, 1386-1446. By Antonio Marescotti, sculptor, of Ferrara.

921. BARTOLOMEO COLLEONE, Condottiere of Bergamo, 1400-1475. By M. Guidizani.

922. FILIPPO MASERANO. Venetian poet. Circa 1457. By Giovanni Boldu.

923. NICHOLAS SCHLIFER. Musician. By GIOVANNI Boldu. 1457.

924. TADDEO MANFREDI, Count of Faenza and Lord of Imola, 1449-1493. By Gian-francesco Enzola, of Parma.

925. FRANCESCO SFORZA, 4th Duke of Milan, 1401-1466. By Enzola.

926. COSTANZO SFORZA, Lord of Pesaro, 1448-1483. By Enzola.

927. GINEVRA SFORZA, wife of Giovanni II. Bentivoglio, of Bologna, and sister of Costanzo Sforza, 1464-1507. Lead.

928. NICCOLO PALMIERI, Bishop of Orte, 1402-1467. By Guazzalotti, of Prato.

929. CALIXTUS III. (Alfonso Borgio), Pope (1455-1458). By Guazzalotti.

930. Pius II. (Piccolomini), Pope, 1458-1464. By Guazzalotti.

931. Sixtus IV. (Francesco della Rovere, Pope, 1471-1484. By Guazzalotti.

932. Cristoforo Moro, Doge of Venice, 1462-1471.

933. Bartolomeo Roverella, Cardinal of Ravenna, 1416-1476.

934. Alexander VI. (Borgia), Pope, 1492-1503.

935. Raimondo Lavagnoli.

936. Cosmo de' Medici, the Elder, 1389-1464.

937. Lorenzo de' Medici, "Il Magnifico," 1448-1492. By Niccolo Fiorentino.

938. Federigo del Montefeltro, 1st Duke of Urbino, 1422-1482. Plaquette.

939. Marsilio Ficino, of Florence, Philosopher, 1433-1499.

940. Girolamo Savonarola, 1452-1498. Attributed to Ambrogio della Robbia.

941. The same. Cast in lead from the intaglio by Giovanni delle Corniole.

942. Gianfrancesco Gonzaga, Lord of Sabbionetta. 1443-1496.

943. Antonia de' Balzi, wife of Gianfrancesco. M. 1479. By P. Jacopo Ilario called L'Antico.

944. Virgilio Malvezzi, noble of Bologna, 1478. By Sperandio, of Mantua.

945. Christian I., King of Denmark, on his visit to Rome in 1474. By Bartolommeo Melioli, of Mantua.

946. Gianfrancesco II., Gonzaga, 4th Marquis of Mantua, 1466-1519. By Melioli.

947. Smaller medal, by the same.

948. Lodovico III., Gonzaga, 2nd Marquis of Mantua, 1414-1478. Bell metal. By Melioli.

949. LODOVICO GONZAGA, Bishop of Mantua, 1458-1511. By Melioli.

950. MATHIAS CORVINUS, King of Hungary, 1443-1490.

951. CHARLES VIII., King of France, 1470-1498.

952. BERAUD STUART, Lord of Aubigny, a Scotchman in the service of Charles VIII., whom he accompanied into Italy. *Circ.* 1494.

953. GIOVANNI GIOVIANO PONTANO. Poet. Was secretary to Ferdinand I., King of Naples. 1426-1503.

954. GIOVANNI II. Bentivoglio, of Bologna, 1443-1509. By Francesco Francia.

955. ROBERTO MOROSINI. Attributed to Francia.

956. JULIUS II. (Giuliano della Rovere). Pope. 1503-1513. Attributed to Francia.

957. The same. By Ambrogio Foppa, called Caradosso.

958. BRAMANTE DA URBINO, Architect, 1446-1514. By Caradosso.

959. FRANCESCO SFORZA, 4th Duke of Milan, 1401-1466. By Caradosso.

960. LODOVICO MARIA SFORZA ("Il Moro"), 7th Duke of Milan, son of Francesco Sforza, 1451-1508. By Caradosso.

961. The same. Small medal in cameo form. Presumably by the same.

962. ASCANIO MARIA SFORZA, Cardinal, 1445-1505. Attributed to Caradosso.

963. NICCOLO ORSINI, Count of Petigliano and Nola, 1442-1540.

964. MAXIMILIAN I., Emperor of Germany, 1459-1519.

965. MARY OF BURGUNDY ; d. of Charles the Bold, first wife of Maximilian I., married in 1477.

966. BORGHESE BORGHESI, of Siena. Born 1414.

967. JACOPO SANNAZZARO (Actius Syncerus), of Naples. Poet. 1458-1530.

968. AGOSTO DA UDINE. Poet (Laureate) and Astrologer. End of 15th Century.

969. NICCOLO TEMPE, of Tarentum.

970. ALBERTO PIO DI CARPI, Count of Carpi, 1475-1531.

971. HORTENSIA PICCOLOMINI, of Siena, 1500-1525.

972. BALDASSARE CASTIGLIONE, of Mantua, 1472-1529.

973. MATTIA UGONI, of Brescia. Bishop of Famagusta. Died 1516.

974. EUSTACHIO BOIANO. Born 1463.

975. FRANCESCO ALIDOSI, Cardinal (1505). Attributed to Francia.

976. EMILIA PIO, wife of Antonio del Montefeltro. *Circa* 1510.

977. GONSALVO OF CORDOVA. "The Great Captain." 1443-1515.

978. GIOVANNI DE' MEDICI ("delle bande nere"), 1498-1526.

979. PIETRO GRIMANI, son of Antonio Grimani, Doge of Venice. (1521-1523). Knight of St. John of Jerusalem.

980. ANDREA GRITTI, Procurator of St. Mark's in 1509; Doge of Venice, 1523-1532.

981. JACOPA DA CORREGIO, 1500-1525.

982. Frederick III., Emperor of Germany, 1415-1493. A retrospective medal, by Antonio Abondio.

983. LOUIS XII., King of France. Born 1462. King in 1498-1515.

984. FRANCIS, Count of Angoulême. Aged 20; afterwards Francis I. of France. 1494-1547.

985. FRANCIS I., of France.

986. The same. By Giovanni Maria Pomedello, of Verona.

987. CHARLES V., when King of Spain (1516-1519) ; afterwards Emperor of Germany. By Pomedello.

988. ISABELLA SESSA, wife of Giovanni Michieli, of Venice. By Pomedello.

989. GIROLAMO CORNARO. Attributed to Andrea Riccio.

990. AGOSTINO LANDO. One of the conspirators who killed Pietro L. Farnese in 1547.

991. PIETRO ANTONIO DEL CASTELLO, 1515.

992. CHRISTINA OF DENMARK, wife of Francesco II. Sforza. Refused marriage with Henry VIII. of England. Dated 1533.

993. PIERRE BRIÇONNET, 1503.

994. FERNANDO FRANCESCO D'AVALOS, Marquis of Pescaro, 1489-1525.

995. ALOYSIUS RIZADO, 1500-1525.

996. LODOVICO ARIOSTO, of Reggio. Poet. 1474-1533. By Domenico Poggini.

997. VITTORE GAMBELLO, called Camelio, of Venice. Sculptor and Medallist. Flourished, 1484-1523. By himself.

998. AGOSTINO BARBARIGO, Doge of Venice, 1486-1501. Born 1419. By Camelio.

999. SIXTUS IV., Pope, 1471-1484. By Camelio.

1000. DOMENICO GRIMANI, of Venice. Cardinal. 1463-1523. By Camelio.

1001. BARTOLOMMEO ALVIANO, of Orvieto. Venetian General. Died 1515.

1002. PIETRO BEMBO. Cardinal. Venetian. 1470-1547. By Valerio Vicentino.

1003. The same. Reverse (shown). Pegasus. By Benvenuto Cellini.

1004. SCIPIO BUZAKRENUS, of Padua. 16th Century.

1005. SCARAMUZZA TRIVULZIO, Bishop of Como. Died 1527.

1006. ANDREA CARAFFA, Count of Santa Severina. Viceroy of Naples in 1525.

1007. GIOVANNI DI NALE. *Circ.* 1525.

1008. LEO X. (Giovanni de' Medici), son of Lorenzo the Magnificent. Born 1475. Pope, 1513-1521.

1009. CLEMENT VII. (Giulio de' Medici). Born 1478. Pope 1523-1534. By Giovanni Bernardi da Castel Bolognese.

1010. CHARLES V., Emperor of Germany, 1500-1558. By Giovanni Bernardi.

1011. DANIEL DE HANNA. By Leone Leoni.

1012. FRANCESCO GUICCIARDINI, of Florence. Historian. 1482-1540.

1013. PIETRO ARETINO, 1492-1557. By Alessandro Vittoria.

1014. PIERIO VALERIANO BOLZANI, of Belluna. Scholar and Critic. 1475-1558.

1015. SIGISMUND AUGUSTUS, King of Poland. 1549. By Domenico Veneziano.

1016. ANDREA DORIA. Genoese Admiral. 1466-1550. By Leone Leoni

1017. PHILIP II., King of Spain, 1527-1598. By Leone Leoni.

1018. MICHAELANGELO BUONAROTTI. Aged 88. 1475-1564. By Leone Leoni.

1019. ALFONZO II. D'AVALOS, Marquis of Guastalla. 1502-1546. By Leone Leoni.

1020. MARIA OF ARAGON, his wife, daughter of Ferdinand of Aragon, Duke of Montalto.

1021. MARCO CROTO, 1500-1525.

1022. ALESSANDRO DE' MEDICI, first Duke of Florence, 1510-1537.

1023. ANTONIO MULA, Duke of Crete.   By Andrea Spinelli.   1538.

1024. ANDREA GRITTI.   Doge of Venice (1523-1538).   By Spinelli.

1025. FABIO MIGNANELLI, of Siena, Bishop of Lucera, 1496-1557.

1026. ISABELLA SFORZA, 1503-1561.

1027. GIROLAMO CARDANO, of Pavia.   Physician and philosopher.   1501-1576.

1028. FRANCESCO MERATI, 1525-1550.

1029. PIETRO PLANTANIDA, of Milan, 1525-1550.

1030. MARCO MANTOVA BENAVIDES, of Padua, 1489-1582.   By Martino da Bergamo.

1031. UNKNOWN PORTRAIT.   Encircled with festoons of flowers.   *Circ.* 1550.

1032. RICA, mother of Elia Delatas.   1552.

1033. GIOVANNI, Cardinal of Lorraine, 1498-1550.   Attributed to Benvenuto Cellini.

1034. LIVIA, wife of Marzio Colonna.   Married in 1540.

1035. GIOVANNI BRESSANI OF BERGAMO.   Poet.   Flourished, 1526–1543.

1036. COSMO I. DE' MEDICI, 2nd Duke of Florence, 1519-1574.   By Domenico di Polo.

1037. JEAN PARISOT DE LA VALETTE, Grand Master of the Order of Malta, 1494-1568.   By Marius.

1038. GIOVANNI MORONI, of Milan.   Cardinal in 1542.

1039. GIROLAMO FIGINO, of Milan.

1040. ALESSANDRO BASSIANO AND GIOVANNI CAVINO.   By G. Cavino, of Padua. *Circ.* 1550.   Struck medal.

1041. FEDERIGO II. GONZAGA, 5th Marquis of Mantua, 1519-1530.   Struck medal. Probably by Camelio.

CASE M.

*CRYSTALS, KNIVES, KEYS, BRONZES, &c.   LENT BY GEORGE
SALTING, ESQ.*

1042. CRYSTAL PLAQUE, with intaglio of the Crucifixion at the back, touched with gold, in
silver gilt frame. Probably Milanese. About 1500. From the Spitzer Collection, No. 2,618.

1043. PLAQUE, painted in gold and translucent enamels. Our Lady of the Rosary, surrounded by worshippers. The border is composed of minute scenes from the
life of Christ. Late 16th Century. In silver gilt frame. From the Spitzer Collection, No. 2089.

1044. GLASS PLAQUE, with representation of the Nativity in etched gold leaf. Early 14th
Century. From the Spitzer Collection, No. 2,088.

1045. PAX, with miniature painting in gold and enamel of St. Jerome and St. Mary
Magdalen. In jewelled frame. North Italian. 15th Century. From the Spitzer
Collection, No. 2,090.

1046. PENDANT, with miniature painting of St. Jerome, in gold and enamel colours, pro-
tected by crystal ; enclosed in an oval gold frame. North Italian. About 1500.
From the Spitzer Collection, No. 2,099.

1047. SILVER MEDALLION, decorated in niello on one side with the Virgin and Child, and
on the other with the Mass of St. Gregory. Florentine. About 1470. From
the Spitzer Collection, No. 1,795.

1048. STEEL PADLOCK, with etched engraved pattern. North Italian. 16th Century.
From the Spitzer Collection, No. 895.

1049. INKSTAND, iron damascened gold in arabesque devices. Milanese. 16th Century.
From the Spitzer Collection, No. 2,536.

1050. LEATHER CASE AND COVER with stamped pattern. 15th Century.

1051. KNIFE CASE, covered with leather, and ornamented with medallions.   16th Century. From the Spitzer Collection, No. 849.

1052. PLAQUE, iron repoussé and damascened.   Judith and Holofernes.   Milanese, 16th Century.   From the Spitzer Collection, No. 2,576.

1053. PLAQUE, iron repoussé and gilt.   A man and woman seated and disputing ; Discord appears on the left.   Milanese.   16th Century.   From the Spitzer Collection, No. 2,577.

1054. LARGE KNIFE, short handle of copper, with horn and mother-of-pearl decoration. 15th Century.   From the Spitzer Collection, No. 2,323.

1055. KNIFE, with amber handle.   16th Century.   From the Spitzer Collection, No. 2,360.

1056. FORK, with amber handle.   16th Century.   From the Spitzer Collection, No. 2,362.

1057. LARGE KNIFE, engraved blade.   16th Century.   From the Spitzer Collection, No. 2,521.

1058. LEATHER CASE, with knife, fork, and tooth-pick.   16th Century.   From the Spitzer Collection, No. 2,375.

1059. KNIFE, mother-of-pearl and gilt handle.   1586.   From the Spitzer Collection, No. 2,425.

1060. KNIFE, mother-of-pearl handle, surmounted by a lion.   16th Century.   From the Spitzer Collection, No. 2,441.

1061. KNIFE, with handle of nielloed silver.   End of 15th Century.   From the Spitzer Collection, No. 2,433.

1062. FORK AND SPOON, combined, silver gilt.   16th Century.   From the Spitzer Collection, No. 2,527.

1063. STEEL KEY, bow formed of two dolphins.   16th Century.   From the Spitzer Collection, No. 937.

1064. STEEL KEY, bow formed of two dragons.   16th Century.   From the Spitzer Collection, No. 921.

BRONZES.

1065. BRONZE FIGURE OF HERCULES, resting 'on club and holding apple of the Hesperides. 15th Century.

1066. BRONZE FIGURE OF ST. SEBASTIAN. 16th Century.

1067. BRONZE FIGURE OF HORSE, being a study in miniature for the horse in the equestrian group of Cosmo de' Medici in the Piazza della Signoria at Florence. By Giovanni da Bologna.

1068. BRONZE GROUP. Hercules slaying the Nemæan lion, which he seizes by the jaw, his knees on its back.

1069. BRONZE FIGURE OF A SPINARIO, youth extracting thorn from his foot.

1070. BRONZE FIGURE OF MELEAGER.

1071. BRONZE FIGURE OF VENUS, seated on a rock.

1072. BRONZE FIGURE OF AN ATHLETE.

1073. BRONZE FIGURE OF VULCAN.

1074. BRONZE FIGURE OF THE FARNESE HERCULES.

1075. BRONZE FIGURE OF VENUS, standing, her left arm outstretched.

1076. BRONZE FEMALE FIGURE, seated.

1077. BRONZE FIGURE OF BACCHUS, pouring wine from a jug.

1078. BRONZE GROUP OF VENUS AND CUPID, riding on d olphins.

1079. BRONZE GROUP OF ADONIS, asleep, resting right foot on boar; at his side, dog.

1080. BRONZE GROUP OF VENUS AND ADONIS, in front, dead boar; behind, dog.

1081. BRONZE GROUP OF CHARITY, holding child in her arms; two other children at her side.

1082. BRONZE GROUP OF DIANA AND DOG.

1083. BRONZE GROUP OF VENUS AND CUPID.

1084. BRONZE TRIPOD INKSTAND, with dolphin legs, and decorated with heads of amorini.

1085. BRONZE VASE, decorated with vine leaves, grapes and flowers. The vase is inscribed, PETRUS EJUSQUE FILIUS FRANCISCUS CAVADINI FUSORES VERONENSES. 16th Century.

1086. FIGURE OF HERCULES about to slay the Nemæan Lion. Italian; middle 16th Century.

Lent by H. PFUNGST, ESQ.

1087. BUST OF MINERVA. Bronze. 16th Century.

Lent by T. WHITCOMBE GREENE, ESQ.

1088. AN OLIVE WOOD TABLE, richly inlaid with ivory and mother-of-pearl ornaments.

Lent by EDWARD HEYWOOD, ESQ.

1089. FIGURE OF PERSEUS, right arm raised; left hand on shield bearing the head of Medusa. Attributed to Gulielmo della Porta. Florentine; middle 16th Century.

Lent by H. PFUNGST, ESQ.

1090. FIGURE OF A YOUTH, kneeling on right knee and supporting a shell (used for a lamp) on his shoulder. Bronze. 15th Century.

Lent by T. WHITCOMBE GREENE, ESQ.

1091. BRONZE FIGURE OF PERSEUS.

Lent by WILLIAM BOORE, ESQ.

1092. BRONZE MORTAR, decorated with arms.

Lent by CHARLES BUTLER, ESQ.

1093. BRONZE STATUETTE of a man drawing a sword. By Giovanni da Bologna.

Lent by the EARL OF WEMYSS.

1094. BRONZE JAR.

Lent by the EARL OF WEMYSS.

CENTRAL HALL.

CASE N.

MAJOLICA.

1095. CASTEL DURANTE PLATE. A coat of arms in the deep sunken centre of the plate. The wide outside rim decorated with arms and trophies, and a label bearing the date 1530 in white and light brown on a deep blue ground.

Lent by HENRY PFUNGST, ESQ.

1096. URBINO TAZZA. Portrait of a young woman wearing laced collar, deep blue gown, and on a scroll behind the name "Laura Bella."

Lent by HENRY PFUNGST, ESQ.

1097. GUBBIO TAZZA. On a deep blue ground are painted arms, dolphins, cornucopia, all richly lustred in ruby, gold, and other colours. About 1525.

Lent by HENRY PFUNGST, ESQ.

1098. URBINO TAZZA. Profile bust of a warrior looking to the left ; he wears a breast-plate and a helmet adorned with grotesque masks. Behind him is a scroll inscribed "Palamed." Outlined and shaded in blue and touched with green, red, and yellow, all relieved against a deep blue ground.

Lent by HENRY PFUNGST, ESQ.

1099. CASTEL DURANTE PLATE. Dragons, arms, &c., in reddish brown and yellow upon a deep blue background. An early specimen dated 1520.

Lent by HENRY PFUNGST, ESQ.

1100. URBINO EWER. Moses striking the rock ; a spirited composition of eleven figures ; the mask under the handle is of unusually good execution.

Lent by HENRY PFUNGST, ESQ.

I

1101. URBINO FLUTED PLATE. Joseph and his brethren.

Lent by the HON. W. F. B. MASSEY-MAINWARING.

1102. URBINO WARE CISTERN. Trefoil form on lions' feet. The interior painted representing Apollo, Minerva, and the Muses. 16th century.

Lent by G. DONALDSON, ESQ.

1103. CAFFAGIOLO DISH. Medallion, surrounded by rows of conventional ornaments; on a white background stands a warrior in armour, leaning on a sword and contemplating the heads of two enemies, with a landscape in the background. On the outer border are four discs and an interlacing pattern in orange, all upon a yellow background, with minute diapering in black. Incised mark on back. An early plate, probably before 1500.

Lent by HENRY PFUNGST, ESQ.

1104. URBINO EWER. Warrior on horseback. Painted by Orazio Fontana, about 1540. From the Field Collection.

Lent by THOMAS MILLER WHITEHEAD, ESQ.

1105. GUBBIO LUSTRED PLATE, with grotesques and ornaments. Curious mark of a hand holding a halberd. Dated 1515.

Lent by DAVID M. CURRIE, ESQ.

1106. FAENZA DISH on foot, with cupids and children, trophies and arabesques in colours on deep blue ground.

Lent by DAVID M. CURRIE, ESQ.

1107. FAENZA PLATE with heads in four medallions and ornaments on blue and yellow ground. Cupid in the centre.

Lent by DAVID M. CURRIE, ESQ.

1108. CAFFAGIOLO MAJOLICA PLATE.

Lent by CHARLES BUTLER, ESQ.

1109. GUBBIO LUSTRED DISH, with five figures of cripples supposed to be cured of ev spirits and other disorders at the tomb of St. Ubaldus, the patron Saint of Gubbio, dated 1521 on a label at the top of the tomb. The back of the dish dated 1522 and signed by Maestro Giorgio.

Lent by DAVID M. CURRIE, ESQ.

1110. GUBBIO LUSTRED PLATE. Cupid in the centre.
Lent by DAVID M. CURRIE, ESQ.

1111. MAJOLICA TAZZA, with bust of a warrior on blue ground.
Lent by FREDERICK DAVIS, ESQ.

1112. GUBBIO PLATE. Cupid represented flying over a wall; in the background a rich landscape; in front two half-draped females. Richly lustred in ruby, gold and other colours, and signed on the reverse Mo'. Giorgio, 1532.
Lent by HENRY PFUNGST, ESQ.

1113. CASTEL DURANTE PLATE; portrait of a warrior in blue on deep orange background; border of dolphins, pelicans, &c.
Lent by HENRY PFUNGST, ESQ.

1114. URBINO CISTERN, representing Apollo on Parnassus, after Raphael.
Lent by FREDERICK DAVIS, ESQ.

1115. URBINO EWER WITH APOLLO AND MARSYAS. Painted by Orazio Fontana, about 1540. From the Field Collection.
Lent by THOMAS M. WHITEHEAD, ESQ.

1116. URBINO DISH. Subject :—Abraham washing the angel's feet. Dated 1543. From the Fountaine Collection.
Lent by SAMUEL MONTAGU, ESQ., M.P.

1117. PUERPERA DISH. Painted inside with figures and bands of foliage; the outside with Cupid.
Lent by CHARLES BUTLER, ESQ.

1118. URBINO DISH. Subject :—Europa. From the Fountaine Collection.
Lent by SAMUEL MONTAGU, ESQ, M.P.

1119. CASTEL DURANTE (?) PLATE. A Cupid surrounded by masks and musical instruments in brownish outline on a yellow ground; the outside border with fruit, in bright colours upon a deep blue ground. The border of this plate, though of a somewhat later date, corresponds in design and colour with that of the fine dish in the South Kensington Museum with the portrait of Perugino, and it is, therefore, probable that this plate emanates from Castel Durante rather than Urbino.
Lent by HENRY PFUNGST, ESQ.

I 2

1120. FAENZA TAZZA. In the centre St. Jerome praying; in green and yellow on a deep blue background : border of arabesques. Dated 1515.

Lent by HENRY PFUNGST, ESQ.

1121. URBINO PLATE. Diana surprised by Actæon ; a coat of arms in the centre.

Lent by HENRY PFUNGST, ESQ.

1122. CAFFAGIOLO PHARMACY JUG. From the Latour Collection.

Lent by ALFRED DE PASS, ESQ.

1123. URBINO CISTERN. Subject :—Adam and Eve being sent out of Eden. Surrounded by grotesque figures. From the Fountaine Collection.

Lent by SAMUEL MONTAGU, ESQ., M.P.

1124. CAFFAGIOLO PLATE. In the centre, surrounded by a band of ornament, "bianco sopra bianco," is the Martyrdom of St. Sebastian, after Francia. Border of arabesques, and a label bearing the date 1520, all symmetrically disposed in the four quarters of the plate ; in white, on a ground of deep blue, and touched with yellow, red, and green. The back decorated with a radiating pattern, outlined in blue and yellow, and a mask in the centre.

Lent by HENRY PFUNGST, ESQ.

1125. GUBBIO TAZZA. Portrait of Giulia Farnese, sister of Pope Paolo III. Face in profile ; she wears a low dress with high embroidered collar. Outlined in blue and on a green background ; border of gold lustre, with honeysuckle ornaments in black, and interwoven the name " Iulia." Early specimen of Maëstro Giorgio ; probably about 1500.

Lent by HENRY PFUNGST, ESQ.

1126. CASTEL DURANTE TAZZA. In the centre an amorino supporting a basket of fruit ; around are trophies of musical instruments, &c., on blue background. Dated 1530.

Lent by HENRY PFUNGST, ESQ.

1127. FAENZA OR FORLI COVER OF A VASE. The upper surface covered with grotesques, and inside the cup is a bird ; all outlined and shaded in blue ; in white on blue background.

Lent by HENRY PFUNGST, ESQ.

1128. CASTEL DURANTE PLATE. A Cupid walking. Border of medallions with beads ; between heads of amorini.
Lent by HENRY PFUNGST, ESQ.

1129. PLATE. The sunken centre and the border decorated with trophies of arms in bluish-grey ; blue background.
Lent by HENRY PFUNGST, ESQ.

1130. URBINO PLATE. The History of Hero and Leander. Signed F. X. (Fra Xanto), 1534 ; a rare date of this master.
Lent by HENRY PFUNGST, ESQ.

1131. FAENZA TAZZA. The Poets on Mount Parnassus, after Raphael's fresco in the Vatican ; the doorway is shown below, and a coat of arms (probably " Salviati ") is added on a tree above painted on a greyish-blue ground. Scrolls in deep blue on the back and in the centre ; on a label the date 1531.
Lent by HENRY PFUNGST, ESQ.

1132. URBINO PLATE. Hercules and Dejanira ; a Coat of Arms suspended from a tree.
Lent by HENRY PFUNGST, ESQ.

1133. URBINO DISH. Hannibal Crossing the Alps ; one of a series of dishes, five of which are in the British Museum, and attributed to Francesco Durantino. From the Bale Collection.
Lent by HENRY PFUNGST, ESQ.

1134. URBINO PLATE. History of the Golden Fleece. Signed "fabula."
Lent by HENRY PFUNGST, ESQ.

1135. GUBBIO PLATE. Abraham and Isaac on their way to the sacrifice. Landscape with wooded hills and a lake, gold and ruby lustres. Dated and signed on the back " Mo. Go. (Maëstro Giorgio), 1522."
Lent by HENRY PFUNGST, ESQ.

1136. URBINO PLATE. Subject from the History of the Foundation of Rome. School of Fra Xanta.
Lent by HENRY PFUNGST, ESQ.

1137. FAENZA TAZZA. St. Jerome in the Desert. After the engraving by Albrecht Dürer. Signed in front " F.R."
Lent by HENRY PFUNGST, ESQ.

1138. URBINO TAZZA. Joseph interpreting Pharaoh's dreams of the lean and fat kine. By Nicolà da Urbino. From the Fountaine Collection.

Lent by HENRY PFUNGST, ESQ.

1139. FAENZA PLATE. Adam and Eve. After Raphael. Dated 1542.

Lent by HENRY PFUNGST, ESQ.

1140. GUBBIO PLATE. Cupid winged, and with his arms tied; painted in grisaille, and touched with ruby lustre on a deep blue background. Painted with gold and ruby lustres on a deep and lustrous blue background. A work of Maëstro Giorgio, probably about 1520.

Lent by HENRY PFUNGST, ESQ.

1141. URBINO TAZZA. Joseph sold by his Brethren. Reverse decorated with amorini flying in clouds, on a wavy blue ground. A fine piece, probably by Orazio Fontana.

Lent by HENRY PFUNGST, ESQ.

1142. URBINO DISH. Joseph before Pharaoh. Triple border of arabesques, birds, cameos, &c. Probably by Orazio Fontana.

Lent by HENRY PFUNGST, ESQ.

1143. URBINO VASE, with snake handles, representing Moses striking the rock. From the Fountaine Collection.

Lent by FREDERICK DAVIS, ESQ.

1144. CASTEL DURANTE DISH. Jupiter and Hebe. Border of "bianco sopra bianco," and edge with arabesque designs in grey on blue ground. Dated 1532.

Lent by HENRY PFUNGST, ESQ.

1145. URBINO DISH. Philip V. of Macedon flying from the Romans; a Bishop's coat of arms suspended from a tree in the centre. In the manner of Francesco Durantino. From the Fountaine Collection.

Lent by HENRY PFUNGST, ESQ.

1146. URBINO DISH. Painted with battle scene. By Orazio Fontana. 16th century.

Lent by G. DONALDSON, ESQ.

1147. BOTTLE, of Sgraffiato ware. Late 16th century.

Lent by HENRY WILLETT, ESQ.

1148. CAFFAGIOLO MAJOLICA DISH, painted with coat of arms of the Gonzaga family ; on raised sevenfoil centre with arabesque ornaments in colour on dark yellow ground.

Lent by CHARLES BUTLER, ESQ.

1149. PESARO or DIRUTA LUSTRED DISH. St. Francis receiving the Stigmata.

Lent by the Hon. W. F. B. MASSEY-MAINWARING.

CASE O.

ARMOUR.

1150. A COMPLETE CHANFRON. The edges are finely engraved with arabesques and scrolls, the front is ornamented with a shield emblazoned with the arms of the Farnese family surmounted by a crown and a spirally fluted spike. The whole is studded with copper gilt nails. Middle of 16th century.

Lent by GUY FRANCIS LAKING, ESQ.

1151. A HORN POWDER-FLASK AND SPANNER, combined, mounted in metal, gilt, chased with beads, fruit and strap ornaments, and with small figure of a monkey. Middle of 16th century.

Lent by MESSRS. DURLACHER BROS.

1152. A PAIR OF FLUTED AND GILT MILANESE MITTEN GAUNTLETS, engraved with floral scrolls. About 1520. From the Fountaine Collection.

Lent by LORD AMHERST OF HACKNEY.

1153. A SIX-SIDED STEEL SPANNER AND PRIMER combined ; with pierced gothic work and spring formed as a bird. End 16th century.

Lent by W. H. SPILLER, ESQ.

1154. A POIGNARD, with pierced pommel and quillons. 12½ inches long.

Lent by GUY FRANCIS LAKING, ESQ.

1155. A FLORENTINE POIGNARD entirely of steel ; the grip is spirally fluted ; the pommel and quillons end in ribbed rosettes ; the blade is 8 inches long and triangular in section. Late 16th century.

Lent by GUY FRANCIS LAKING, ESQ.

1156. ANOTHER POIGNARD, nearly similar, engraved with scrolls.   10 inches long.

Lent by GUY FRANCIS LAKING, ESQ.

1157. ANOTHER POIGNARD, inlaid with small bands of silver.   8¾ inches long.

Lent by GUY FRANCIS LAKING, ESQ.

1158. A SMALL WHEEL LOCK PISTOL, entirely of steel, with six-sided pommel, minutely engraved with a hound and scrolls.   Middle 16th century.

Lent by W. H. SPILLER, ESQ.

1159. A STILETTO, entirely of steel, with fluted quillons, triangular grooved blade, 6½ inches long, with steel mounted sheath.   Late 16th century.

Lent by W. H. SPILLER, ESQ.

1160. A STILETTO, entirely of steel, spirally fluted grip, the quillons ending in knobs; triangular blade with receptacles said to be for poisoned salve.   Late 16th century.

Lent by JAMES GURNEY, ESQ.

1161. SIMILAR ONE, plainer.   7 inches long.

Lent by W. H. SPILLER, ESQ.

1162. PATRON BOX OF STEEL, entirely engraved with birds, hounds and scrolls.   Middle 16th century.

Lent by W. H. SPILLER, ESQ.

1163. A HORN FLASK, with Mars and Venus mounted in bronze.   16th Century.

Lent by MESSRS. DURLACHER BROS.

1164 A TOE OF A SOLERETTE of bright steel, embossed with masks and scrolls.   Middle 16th century.

Lent by T. FOSTER SHATTOCK, ESQ.

1165. A DAGGER, fluted quillons and pommel, pierced and serrated blade, 6¾ inches long.   Meyrick collection.   16th century.

Lent by JAMES GURNEY, ESQ.

1166. A DAGGER with single ring, straight quillons and faceted pommel, damascened with scrolls in gold and silver; pierced and channelled blade, 10 inches long.   Middle 16th century.

Lent by JAMES GURNEY, ESQ.

1167. CIRCULAR SHIELD OF STEEL, repoussé with figures and arabesques on gold ground on six bands in the centre, the border arabesques, animals, flowers, &c., with original velvet lining. 16th century.

Lent by DAVID M. CURRIE, ESQ.

1168. DAGGER. The hilt is of Italian workmanship, the pommel of spherical form and the quillons ending in knobs, decorated with finely-chased and gilt rosettes. The blade has two pierced groves and bears on its recasso the letter G, the mark of Giraldo Ruiz of Toledo. 16 inches long. Late 16th century.

Lent by GUY FRANCIS LAKING, ESQ.

1169. CASQUE, with plume-holder, triple ridge, and support for plume, repoussé, with fleur-de-lys, mask and ornaments. Part of the armour of an officer of Cosmo de' Medici. 16th century. From the Londesborough Collection.

Several casques of this same design exist in the Royal Armouries at Turin and Capo di Monte ; and one in the Meyrick Collection (*Skelton, plate* 32) was attributed, and probably rightly, to the body-guard of Cosmo de' Medici, Duke of Florence (A.D. 1537–1574).

Lent by DAVID M. CURRIE, ESQ.

1170. A MORION, engraved with trophies of arms and bands and four circular medallions with heads ; it has the original spikes with embossed and engraved plume-holder ; gilt.

Lent by JAMES GURNEY, ESQ.

1171. EMBOSSED CASQUE of classic form entirely forged from one piece. It is of Italian workmanship of russet and gold with fluted and corded comb and peak. The sides are decorated with a full faced head and acanthus foliage springing from the Florentine fleur-de-lys. The neck and ear plates are ornamented with budding floral scrolls. The whole work is raised and gilt on a russet ground. End of 16th century.

Lent by GUY FRANCIS LAKING, ESQ.

1172. MILANESE LEFT-HANDED DAGGER, with octagonal pommel, diamond-shaped quillons and single ring. The whole is richly damascened with gold and silver azziminia. The blade is stiff and four-sided, and bears the armourer's mark on the ricasso, 12½ inches long. Late 16th century.

Lent by GUY FRANCIS LAKING, ESQ.

1173. A LONG DAGGER with single ring, curved quillons and shaped pommel decorated with rosettes.-Pierced and channelled blade, 14½ inches long ; the grip inlaid with mother-of-pearl and stained ivory, Middle 16th century.

> Lent by W. H. SPILLER, ESQ.

1174. A TASSET and part of a pauldron of a page's suit, puffed and slashed, engraved with scrolls and gilt. Early 16th century.

> Lent by JAMES GURNEY, ESQ.

1175. DAGGER, fluted pommel and straight quillons, inlaid with small bands of silver with channelled and finely pierced blade, 8¾ inches long. Middle 16th century.

> Lent by W. H. SPILLER, ESQ.

1176. A CURVED SPANNER AND PRIMER of ivory, finely engraved with a hunt ; birds and scrolls mounted in gilt steel work. Middle 16th century.

> Lent by W. H. SPILLER, ESQ.

1177. SHIELD OF RUSSET STEEL of the finest workmanship, repoussé and damascened in gold. In the centre a Roman Emperor and a soldier outside a tent ; above a large female mask and underneath a grotesque mask of a satyr ; the border composed of two chained captives, trophies and fruit. 16th century.

> Lent by DAVID M. CURRIE, ESQ.

1178. TWO ELBOW PIECES or COUDES of bright steel embossed with flowers, scrolls &c., the borders damascened with scrolls in gold, probably the work of Negroli. These were worn with chain mail and attached to the pauldrons by scaled bands, as seen in these examples. Middle 16th century. From the Fountaine Collection.

> Lent by JAMES GURNEY, ESQ.

1179. POWDER FLASK of cuir bouilli, fluted and with a shield and two lions mounted in gilt iron. 16th century.

> Lent by W. H. SPILLER, ESQ.

1180. HORN POWDER FLASK, engraved with a deer and foliage, mounted in iron gilt. End of the 16th century.

> Lent by W. H. SPILLER, ESQ.

1181. PAIR OF STEEL GAUNTLETS, repoussé, damascened with gold ; in the centre of each
is a figure of Mars, with captives and trophies at the sides. Part of the same
suit as the preceding. From the Bernal and Londesborough Collections. 16th
century.

Lent by DAVID M. CURRIE, ESQ.

1182. BREASTPLATE of steel, repoussé work, richly damascened with gold ; gilt background
and inlaid with silver. In the centre at top a Gorgon's head, beneath two captives seated on an arch supported by terminal figures, and a statue of Mars resting
on the heads of two Fauns ; on either side festoons and masks, medallions of
Jupiter, Mercury, Saturn, Apollo, Trophies, Satyrs, &c. This breastplate is said
to have been worn by Philip IV. of Spain. From the Bernal and Londesborough
Collections. 16th century.

Lent by DAVID M. CURRIE, ESQ.

CASE P.

ARMOUR.

1183. A CIRCULAR SHIELD OF BRIGHT STEEL, engraved with three bands radiating from
the centre, with St. George and the Dragon, lions, griffins and terminal figures ;
between, are two circular medallions with winged snakes in scroll borders ; the
edge is engraved with a border of griffins, lions, figures and scrolls. Early part
of 16th century.

Lent by SAMUEL WILLSON, ESQ.

1184. MILANESE CUP-HILTED RAPIER, the quillons and knuckle-guard spirally fluted and
ornamented with bands of foliage. The cup is finely pierced with two borders of
scroll foliage ; the edge is heavily rolled to catch the point of the adversary's
rapier. The blade is 40 ins. long, and the recasso is covered with the original
leather.

Lent by GUY FRANCIS LAKING, ESQ.

1185. A GAUNTLET, partly ribbed, with steel rivets. Close of 15th century.

Lent by W. H. SPILLER, ESQ.

1186. ANOTHER, similar.

Lent by W. H. SPILLER, ESQ.

1187. A COUDE or elbow piece. *Circa* 1410.

Lent by GUY FRANCIS LAKING, ESQ.

1188. A HAUBERK OF MAIL; each link is rivetted. It is of great weight—20 lbs—intended for use before plated armour was fully developed. About 1400.

Lent by GUY FRANCIS LAKING, ESQ.

1189. A SWEPT HILTED RAPIER, with straight quillons, minutely inlaid with small grains of silver, four-sided blade.

Lent by W. H. SPILLER, ESQ.

1190. PRODD (arabalête-à-jalet) or cross-bow for sporting purposes made to shoot small bullets. The wood is of Italian walnut carved with two panels of griffins and acanthus foliage, the butt is carved with a grotesque mask, &c., the bow and trigger-guard are floriated and fluted. The foresight (between which a bead was suspended on a silk thread) is in the form of two small classical columns, and has a movable back sight. 36 inches long; stretch of bow 22½ inches. Middle of 16th century.

Lent by GUY FRANCIS LAKING, ESQ.

1191. THE BACK OF A GORGET of fine workmanship with borders damascened in gold, and raised silver studs. In the centre a repoussé medallion of a figure leaning on a column. 16th century. From the Londesborough Collection. A helmet of similar quality is in the Museé d'Artillerie, Paris.

Lent by DAVID M. CURRIE, ESQ.

1192. A PRODD OR CROSSBOW for sporting purposes, gilt and chased with animals and ornaments. The butt of wood is inlaid with ivory, and engraved with masks and dolphins. 16th century.

Lent by DAVID M. CURRIE, ESQ.

1193. RAPIER, by Federico Picinino, with octagonal pommel, straight quillons, knuckle-guard and pas d'ane. Inlaid with small circles in silver. Four sided blade stamped on the recasso with armourer's mark. Length of blade, 39½ inches. 16th century.

Lent by W. H. SPILLER, ESQ.

CASE R.

EMBROIDERIES, NEEDLEWORK AND LACE.

1212. BORDER, floral design
Lent by LORD BATTERSEA.

1213. BLUE SILK CUSHION, embroidered with the arms of the Pallavicini family.
Lent by STUART M. SAMUEL, ESQ.

1214. JEWELLED BANNER, with arms of the Confraternity of the Trinita, floral design on white silk ground
Lent by LORD BATTERSEA.

1215. ALTAR FRONTAL. Shaded silver and silk embroidery on blue silk; figure of St. Joseph and Infant Christ in centre; faces painted.
Lent by CHARLES BUTLER, ESQ.

1216. ALTAR FRONTAL, richly embroidered with a representation of a garden of flowers
1 in raised gold, silver, and coloured silks upon silk embroidered ground. 16th century.
Lent by STUART M. SAMUEL, ESQ.

1217. FLORAL DESIGN on white, inlaid stitches, figure of serpent appliqué.
Lent by CHARLES BUTLER, ESQ.

1218. BORDER; arabesque design on gold worked ground.
· Lent by CHARLES BUTLER, ESQ.

1219. EMBROIDERED PANEL; St. Michael, worked in silks on raised gold ground.
Lent by CHARLES BUTLER, ESQ.

1220. CHALICE VEIL. Design of flowers and birds; ground worked in silver.
Lent by CHARLES BUTLER, ESQ.

1221. CHALICE VEIL. Raised gold and silver arabesques and coloured silk flowers on white silk.
Lent by CHARLES BUTLER, ESQ.

1222. BORDER. Floral design.
Lent by LORD BATTERSEA.

1223. TEXTILE—WOVEN GOLD AND SILVER THREAD.
Lent by CHARLES BUTLER, ESQ.

1224. CREDENCE CLOTH. Border of coloured silk, lace embroidery.
Lent by CHARLES ROWLEY, ESQ.

1225. PIECE OF PUNTO REALE. Design by Babella Catanea Parasole at Rome, 1600.
Lent by LADY LAYARD.

1226. FLORENTINE LACE. 14th century.
Lent by ARTHUR LUCAS, ESQ.

1227. SPECIMEN OF FINE SILK EMBROIDERY ON LINEN.
Lent by L. BEST, ESQ.

1228. SILK DARNED NET EMBROIDERY.
Lent by L. BEST, ESQ.

1229. SILK DARNED NET EMBROIDERY.
Lent by L. BEST, ESQ.

1230. CREDENCE CLOTH. White linen, coloured satin stitch embroidery.
Lent by CHARLES ROWLEY, ESQ.

1231. SILVER LACE.
Lent by LORD BATTERSEA.

1232. CREDENCE CLOTH. Shaded gold embroidery and coloured silk.
Lent by CHARLES ROWLEY, ESQ.

1233. STRIP OF GOLD AND SILVER LACE.
Lent by LORD BATTERSEA.

1234. LACE BORDER FOR VESTMENT. Point de Milan. 16th century.
Lent by the Right Rev. the BISHOP OF PORTSMOUTH.

235. SPECIMENS OF GOLD LACE ON CUT LINEN.
Lent by L. BEST, ESQ.

1236. COLOURED SILK EMBROIDERY ON DRAWN NET.
Lent by L. BEST, ESQ.

1237. CREDENCE CLOTH. Arabesque border in gold and silk embroidery.
Lent by CHARLES ROWLEY, ESQ.

1238. WHITE SILK CHASUBLE. Embroidered in flat gold and coloured silks.

Lent by CHARLES BUTLER, ESQ.

1239. RED COPE. Gold and silver brocade, pineapple design.

Lent by CHARLES BUTLER, ESQ.

1240. GREEN SILK EMBROIDERED BORDER.

Lent by MRS. H. E. GORDON.

1241. COPE of green Genoese velvet.

Lent by CHARLES BUTLER, ESQ.

1242. DRAWN THREAD WORK—opus filatorium—with coloured silk darning.

Lent by MRS. H. E. GORDON.

1243. COPE—white and silver brocade—embroidered in gold, silver, and coloured gold thread. Figure of St. Francis of Assisi on hood.

Lent by CHARLES BUTLER, ESQ.

1244. YELLOW SILK COVERLET, embroidered in metal threads.

Lent by CHARLES BUTLER, ESQ.

1245. PANEL, embroidered arabesque in coloured silks on yellow ground.

Lent by MRS. H. E. GORDON.

1246. ALTAR FRONTAL embroidered in laid gold and coloured silks on white satin. Figure of saint in centre.

Lent by CHARLES BUTLER, ESQ.

1247. BLUE LINEN COVER worked in silks.

Lent by CHARLES BUTLER, ESQ.

1248. PYX CLOTH in "nun's work."

Lent by C. FAIRFAX MURRAY, ESQ.

1249. ALTAR FRONTAL. White silk embroidered in laid stitches. Figure of St. Anthony with Infant Christ in centre. Roman eagle, foliage design.

Lent by WICKHAM FLOWER, ESQ.

1250. COVERLET, white silk, foliage design, embroidered in coloured silks.

Lent by LORD BATTERSEA.

K

1251. PANEL. Floral design. Ground Punta Francese.

Lent by MRS. H. E. GORDON.

1252. PANEL. Blue silk ground, floral design embroidered in silver and coloured silks.

Lent by MISS HALLÉ.

1253. FLORAL ARABESQUE in coloured silks and gold on white worked ground.

Lent by CHARLES ROWLEY, ESQ.

1254. COPE, white satin embroidered in laid gold and coloured silks, floral design.

Lent by CHARLES BUTLER, ESQ.

1255. COPE OF CLOTH OF GOLD made in Florence. Early 16th century. The orphrey and hood probably of English origin and added at a later period. *Testamenta Vetusta ed. Nicholas t. i. p.* 33, " The whole suit of vestments and coopies of cloth of gold tissue wrought with our badges of red roses and portcullises, the which we of late caused to be made at Florence in Italy, which our King Henry VII. in his will bequeathed to God and St. Peter, and to the Abbot and Priory and Convent of our Monastery of Westminster."

Lent by the RECTOR OF STONYHURST COLLEGE.

1256. COPE. Silver and white damask woven with coloured flowers.

Lent by CHARLES BUTLER, ESQ.

257. YELLOW SILK COVERLET. Reversible embroidery, floral design in colours.

Lent by CHARLES BUTLER, ESQ.

CASE S.

CABINETS, ARMOUR, &c.

1258. CABINET OF MILANESE WORK C. 1540. The entire surface is enriched in a most elaborate style with panels of cartouche work, enclosing classical figures executed in low relief in repoussé, and damascened in every part with a variety of arabesque patterns in gold and silver ; at each angle is a detached iron column standing on a regular pedestal. Inside are drawers, which, together with the falling part, are also enriched in the same elaborate manner. Formerly in the Hamilton Palace Collection.

Lent by JAMES GURNEY, ESQ.

1259. ITALIAN RAPIER, the pommel and guards entirely covered with chased and pierced work representing battle scenes, human figures, animals and busts. The blade has three short grooves. Second half of the 16th century.

Lent by EDWIN M. HODGKINS, ESQ.

1260. SWORD, partly gilt. The circular pommel, grip and quillons chiselled with Emperors' heads in two medallions, figures of warriors, masks and ornaments. The channelled and perforated blade signed I. D. O., and dated 1559.

Lent by DAVID M. CURRIE, ESQ.

1261. SWORD. The pommel, grip, and guard chiselled with figures, masks, medallions, heads, &c., on gold ground, the grip terminating in grotesque heads. 16th century.

Lent by DAVID M. CURRIE, ESQ.

1262. A VIOLIN made by Gaspar da Salo of Brescia. Circa 1580.

Lent by LORD AMHERST OF HACKNEY.

1263. LUTE. Head inlaid in ivory and ebony, with pattern on keyboards. 16th century.

Lent by J. A. FULLER-MAITLAND, ESQ.

1264. A PIECE of embroidery.

Lent by the RIGHT REV. THE BISHOP OF PORTSMOUTH.

1265. AN ALTAR FRONTAL.

Lent by CHARLES BUTLER, ESQ.

1266. AN ALTAR FRONTAL in silk.

Lent by WICKHAM FLOWER, ESQ.

1267. A PIECE of velvet brocade. Genoese.

Lent by LORD BATTERSEA.

1268. PONTIFICAL chair in carved wood gilt, covered with Genoese velvet.

Lent by SIR JULIAN GOLDSMID, BART., M.P.

K 2

1269. BUST of Hadrian in bronze, marble and stucco.   16th century.

Lent by the EARL OF WEMYSS.

1270. CIRCULAR MEDALLION in della Robbia ware.   Representing the Virgin holding on her arm the Infant Saviour, and St. John.

Lent by G. DONALDSON, ESQ.

1271. CRUCIFIX in wood, surmounted by a pelican feeding her young.   Height 48 in.

Lent by LORD BATTERSEA.

1272. BRONZE BUST of Bishop Salutati of Fiesole.   15th century.   By Mino da Fiesole.

Lent by PROF. P. FOSCA.

1273. THE NATIVITY.   Small group in relief with the Holy Ghost and cherubim above, 21½ × 14 in.   By della Robbia.

Lent by HENRY WAGNER, ESQ.

1274. BRONZE BUST of a member of the Strozzi family (?).   From the Strozzi Palace at Florence.

Lent by J. P. HESELTINE, ESQ.

1275. WOOD BUST OF JULIUS CÆSAR.

Lent by ISAAC FALCKE, ESQ.

1276. BRONZE BUST OF HENRY VII.   By Torregiano.

Lent by the EARL OF WEMYSS.

1277. VIRGIN AND CHILD.   By Luca della Robbia.

Lent by LADY TREVELYAN.

1278. CARVED X-SHAPED CHAIR in walnut wood.   1500.

Lent by G. DONALDSON, ESQ.

1279. VIRGIN AND CHILD in gesso duro, 27½ × 18¼ in.

Lent by SIR FREDERICK LEIGHTON, Bart., P.R.A.

1280. MAJOLICA CRUSTED PLATE of Diruta or Pesaro ware, with battle-scene.

Lent by EDMUND OLDFIELD, ESQ.

1281. TWO COPPER WATER POTS.   Tuscan.   Late 16th century.

Lent by SIR JAMES D. LINTON, P.R.I.

1282. CARVED X-SHAPED CHAIR in walnut.

Lent by HAROLD A. PETO, ESQ.

1283. BAS-RELIEF in terra cotta representing the Madonna and Child. Ascribed to Andrea del Verrocchio. Italian; 15th century.
Lent by HENRY PFUNGST, ESQ.

1284. URBINO PLATE with battle-scene. By Orazio Fontana.
Lent by EDMUND OLDFIELD, ESQ.

1285. MARBLE BUST OF ST. JOHN THE BAPTIST in *alto relievo*. By Donatello.
Lent by The Rt. Hon. SIR CHARLES WENTWORTH DILKE, Bart., M.P.

1286. VIRGIN AND CHILD in carta pesta coloured, 20 × 14½ in.
Lent by HENRY WILLETT, ESQ.

1287. A DIRUTA WARE DISH, with figures of two saints and scroll border.
Lent by CHARLES BUTLER, ESQ.

1288. ST. JOHN THE BAPTIST. Half-length profile to left, in high relief, of the youthful St. John the Baptist; marble. By Donatello.
Lent by LORD BATTERSEA.

1289. VIRGIN AND CHILD WITH ST. JOHN, in gesso duro, coloured and gilt, 26 × 17 in.
Lent by the EARL BROWNLOW.

1290. MAJOLICA PLATE, representing the Conversion of St. Paul.
Lent by SIR JULIAN GOLDSMID, BART., M.P.

1291. AN EBONY CABINET, decorated with designs of flowers and birds, in inlaid marbles, columns of lapis lazuli, &c., and surmounted by figures in bronze of amorini. This cabinet formerly belonged to the Medici family.
Lent by CAPT. H. NAYLOR LEYLAND, M.P.

1292. CARVED FIGURE, in wood. Early 16th century.
Lent by ISAAC FALCKE, ESQ.

1293. MARBLE, in high relief, of the Virgin holding the Infant Saviour on her knee. In low relief, in the background, are figures of Angels and heads of Cherubim. By Donatello. 15th century.
Lent by G. DONALDSON, ESQ.

1294. SILVER PLAQUE, after Donatello.

Lent by the EARL OF WEMYSS,

1295. JOB AND HIS WIFE. Within illuminated letter S.

Lent by CHARLES BUTLER, ESQ.

1296. GROUP OF SAINTS. St. Agnes, St. Catherine, and other female saints. Within illuminated letter C.

Lent by CHARLES BUTLER, ESQ.

1297. THE ASCENSION. Within illuminated initial letter P.

Lent by CHARLES BUTLER, ESQ.

1298. THE PENTECOST. Within illuminated letter C.

Lent by CHARLES BUTLER, ESQ.

1299. TWO GROTESQUE HEADS IN RED WAX. By LIONARDO DA VINCI.

Lent by J. LUMSDEN PROPERT, ESQ., M.D.

1300. PAIR OF ENGRAVED METAL CANDLESTICKS.

Lent by FREDERICK DAVIS, ESQ.

1301. EBONY CABINET AND TABLE inlaid with ivory, engraved with mythological subjects, dated 1593.

Lent by WICKHAM FLOWER, ESQ.

1302. PAIR OF BRONZE FIRE-DOGS AND FOUR IRONS with terminal figures with draped heads. 16th century. By Giovanni da Bologna.

Lent by MESSRS. DURLACHER BROS.

1303. CARVED FIGURE, in wood. Early 16th century.

Lent by ISAAC FALCKE, ESQ.

1304. HEAD OF A LAUGHING FAUN. Florentine. Late 15th or early 16th century.

Lent by HENRY PFUNGST, ESQ.

1305. ST. CECILIA, profile to the left. Bas-relief in slate, 21¾ × 15 in. By DONATELLO.

Lent by the EARL OF WEMYSS.

1306. VIRGIN AND CHILD. Coloured bas-relief in gesso duro. 15 × 12½ in.

Lent by HENRY WILLETT, ES Q.

1307. TWO FAUCHARDS DE PARADE. From the Borghese Collection.

Lent by MISS ETHEL FOSTER.

1308. A TWO-HANDED SWORD, with double ring and straight quillons and oviform pommel. The blade is grooved with two small projections near the hilt; fishskin grip. Total length, 5 feet 7¼ inches. Early 16th century.

Lent by W. H. SPILLER, ESQ.

1309. BOAR SPEAR of very curious shape with two lateral projections. It is engraved with oval medallions with classical female figures and is bordered with fine scroll work, the edges of which are gilt—it is fastened to the haft by means of engraved bands and small steel rosettes. 16th century.

Lent by GUY FRANCIS LAKING, ESQ.

1310. RESIDENZA, or Ceremonial Throne of Juliano de' Medici. After the death of Juliano in 1516 it became the property of Count Nuti, attached to the Court of the Medici. It remained in that family until 1872, when it was sold by the Countess Lucrezia Nuti to Prince Demidoff, at whose death in 1881 it was again sold. The authenticity of this superb work of Italian art is attested in a document signed by the director of the Pitti Palace, the Countess Nuti, and four other persons of distinction in Florence, and remains in the possession of the exhibitor. Carved by Baccio D'Agnolo in Florence in the early part of the 16th century.

Lent by G. DONALDSON, ESQ.

1311. CLOSED HELMET OF BLUED STEEL, with high corded comb. Early 16th century.

Lent by W. H. SPILLER, ESQ.

1312. A MORION, engraved with classical equestrian figures, in a border formed of a laurel wreath, the edges engraved with scroll foliage, &c., in gold on blue ground. From the Meyrick collection. Middle 16th century.

Lent by W. H. SPILLER, ESQ.

1313. A CAP À PIE SUIT OF ARMOUR, consisting of breast and back plate, gorget, pauldrons, rere and vam, braces, gauntlets, closed helmet with light corded comb, cuisses, jambs and sollerettes ; the work is engraved with bands of terminal figures, vases and utensils, has been originally gilt, and is studded with copper gilt rivets, with sword with steel and swept hilt.   Middle 16th century.

Lent by SAMUEL WILLSON, ESQ.

1314. A BUCKLER ; the back and front covered with velvet, studded with gilt nails, and has a hook attached for a lantern when used at night.   22 ins. in diameter. Late 16th century.

Lent by SIR JAMES D. LINTON, P.R.I.

1315. MARBLE BUST of a lady of the Piccolomini family, from the Villa Piccolomini, Fojano, near Siena.   Attributed to Nicolo della Guardia, the sculptor of the early Piccolomini tomb in the St. Andrea della Valley, Rome.   1470.

Lent by T. HUMPHRY WARD, ESQ.

SOUTH GALLERY.

CASE T.

ILLUMINATED MANUSCRIPTS.

1316. THE CORONATION OF THE VIRGIN. The Virgin in a mandorla surrounded by angels ; above, Christ with the Apostles holding crown ; above, the Creator. Illuminated page of a manuscript. By Fra Angelico.

Lent by CAPT. G. L. HOLFORD, C.I.E.

1317. GRADUAL (the Ordinary only) of the Church of SS. Cosmo and Damian at Rome. Manuscript on vellum, of the 15th century, of Paduan work. Contains five paintings by Andrea and Francesco Mantegna, and three paintings by another hand, with many illuminated initials and borders. Large folio, in original binding. The painting shown represents the miracle performed by SS. Cosmo and Damian, who, being invoked by a man with a diseased leg. removed it whilst he was in a deep sleep and replaced it by a leg of a Moor, who had just died.

Lent by THOMAS BROOKE, ESQ.

1318. DAVID PLAYING THE HARP ; other figures stand behind. Illuminated initial letter B.

Lent by DAVID M. CURRIE, ESQ.

1319. MANUSCRIPT on pure vellum of the Epistles of St. Paul executed for one of the Medici family. It is ornamented with six miniatures representing Saints Jerome, Paul, James, John, and Jude, and also decorated with intitulations in letters o gold ; 144 capitals and six elegant borders—composed of birds, insects, flowers, and fruit finely illuminated in gold and colours. In green velvet cover with enamelled silver gilt clasps incorporating the Medici arms. 16th century.

Lent by DAVID M. CURRIE, ESQ.

CASE U.

ILLUMINATED MANUSCRIPTS.

1320. LYRA, NICOLAS DE. Postilla super Libros Veteris Testamenti. Manuscript on vellum, with many illuminations.

Three volumes. It was written in the year 1407, and presented to a member of the Malatesta family.

Lent by the EARL OF CRAWFORD, K.T.

CASE V.

ILLUMINATED MANUSCRIPTS.

1321. PETRARCA, FRANCESCO. RIME. Canzoni distese del chiarissimo Poeta Dante Allighieri di Firenze. Folio. Sæc. xiv. on vellum.

Written during the life-time of Petrarch, or immediately after his death, for Lorenzo the son of Carlo degli Strozzi (a member of one of the noblest families of Florence), by Paul the Scribe, as appears by the colophon : *' Gratissimi spetiosique hujus voluminis adepto fiet Laus sit et Gloria Deo qui Laurentio Karoli de Stroççis qui ipsum fieri fecit Pauloque Scriptori ejusdem felicem tribuat vitam per tempora longiora. Amen."* The volume is adorned with large initial letters, and three *illuminated borders*, containing portraits of the Poets and their Inamoratas, executed in the style of Florentine art at that period, with the arms of the Strozzi emblazoned in the bottom compartment of the first two.

From the colophon in which *Laurentius de Strozzis* is called *Filius Karoli* without the ̄*quondam*, the *Beatæ Memoriæ*, or any other *formula* to the same effect, which, no doubt, would have been used at that time in Italy, if Karolus was dead when that colophon was written, it is clear that he was still alive at that moment ; and, as this celebrated Florentine died at a very advanced age in 1383, the volume was written *before* that time, but how long it is difficult to ascertain. All we can say is, that *Lorenzo* (for whom this volume was written) had five sisters, who, as early as the year 1331, were all nuns in the Monastery of St. Dominic at Florence (See Litta), and no doubt he had arrived at the age of manhood, and was quite able to collect fine books long before the year 1383.

Lent by the EARL OF CRAWFORD, K.T.

1322. GIOVANNI CLIMACO, SAN. Incomincia il libro di Sancto Giovanni Climaco della fuga del mondo et della Sancta Scala. Manuscript on vellum, written by an Italian scribe of the 15th century. (10¾ × 8.)

Lent by the EARL OF CRAWFORD, K.T.

1323. CASSIANUS, JOH. SEYTHUS. Libri Collationum Sanctissimorum Patrum. De institutis patrum et de principalibus Vetiis. 4to. Beautiful Italian MS. with many illuminations, circa 140c.

Blue morocco. C. Smith. On vellum. (Libri MSS. 226.)

Lent by the EARL OF CRAWFORD, K.T.

1324. PROLIANO, CHRISTIANO. Compendium Astrologiæ et Astronomiæ. Small Folio. About 1477.

A manuscript of the fifteenth century, written and illuminated by an Italian scribe. The first page is surrounded by a beautiful interlaced border, with birds and amorini introduced. At the foot are the arms of Antonelli (to whom the MS. is dedicated), supported by amorini.

Lent by the EARL OF CRAWFORD, K.T.

1325. VOLUME containing a collection of miniatures of various schools. The miniature exhibited contains representations of Four Evangelists, and has formed part of an Italian (Tuscan) choir-book of the beginning of the 15th century.

Lent by CAPT. G. L. HOLFORD, C.I.E.

1326. MOSES BAR HAEMAN, RABBI. Biur al Htora, Expositio Legis, detto Haramban . . . MS. in Hebrew, rabbinical character and no points. Some fine borders. On vellum. Folio. MS.

Lent by the EARL OF CRAWFORD, K.T.

CASE W.

ILLUMINATED MANUSCRIPTS.

1327. THE HOURS OF OUR LADY (ROMAN USE). Manuscript on vellum, of late 15th century Florentine work. With illuminated borders and numerous miniatures. Small 4to.

Lent by DAVID M. CURRIE, ESQ.

1328. THE ORATIONS OF CICERO. Manuscript on vellum, of late 15th century Florentine work. With illuminated borders and miniatures attributed to Attavante. On the first page are the arms of the Medici family. 8vo.

Lent by MESSRS. ELLIS AND ELVEY.

1329. JURAMENTUM DOMINI ANTONII ERICE PROCURATORIS SANCTI MARCI SEXTE[R]IO[RUM] DE CITRA CANALE. Manuscript on vellum of late 15th century. Veronese work. With an illuminated border, with miniatures and the arms of the Erizzo family of Verona. Small folio.

Lent by SAMUEL SANDARS, ESQ.

1330. THE HOURS OF OUR LADY (ROMAN USE). Manuscript on vellum of the 15th century. Florentine work, with many miniatures and illuminated borders. 3 parts. Small 8vo.

Lent by THOMAS BROOKE, ESQ.

1331. BREVIARY OF THE USE OF THE BENEDICTINE ABBEY OF MONTE CASSINO. Manuscript on vellum, written, probably at Monte Cassino itself, in 1404. Contains many illuminated borders and initials, and fifteen large miniatures. Folio, in original binding.

Lent by THOMAS BROOKE, ESQ.

1332. PART OF A BOOK OF THE HOURS OF OUR LADY, CONTAINING THE OFFICE OF THE DEAD, THE HOURS OF THE PASSION, &C. Manuscript on vellum, of late 15th century Florentine work, of the School of Attavante, with illuminations and miniatures. 16mo.

Lent by DAVID M. CURRIE, ESQ.

1333. HOURS OF OUR LADY OF ROMAN USE. Manuscript on vellum, of Florentine work of the middle of the 15th century, with numerous illuminations and miniatures. 16mo.

Lent by SAMUEL SANDARS, ESQ.

1334. FRANCISCI PETRARCAE POETAE CLARISSIMI TRIUMPHI. The "Trionfi" of Petrarch. Manuscript on vellum, of 16th century, Venetian or Paduan work, with large miniatures and illuminations. Octavo.

Lent by CAPT. G. L. HOLFORD, C.I.E.

1335. EPISTLES AND GOSPELS. Manuscript on vellum, of early 16th century Venetian work, with numerous miniatures and borders, by Benedetto Bordoni, the author of the "Isolario." Folio.

Lent by CAPT. G. L. HOLFORD, C.I.E.

1336. HOURS OF OUR LADY OF ROMAN USE. Manuscript on vellum, of North Italian work of about 1500, with illuminated borders and numerous miniatures. Small 8vo.

Lent by SAMUEL SANDARS, ESQ.

1337. HOURS OF OUR LADY. Manuscript on vellum, of late 15th century, Florentine work, with numerous illuminations and miniatures, and the arms of Lorenzo de' Medici, Cybo, and Salviati. (Maddalena, daughter of Lorenzo, married Francesco Cybo in 1487; another daughter, Lucrezia, married Giacomo Salviati shortly before 1490.) 18mo.

Lent by SAMUEL SANDARS, ESQ.

CASE X.

ILLUMINATED MANUSCRIPTS.

1338. MISSAL. Manuscript on vellum, of early 15th century, South Italian work, with illuminated borders and initials, and miniatures. Folio.

Lent by the DUKE OF ST. ALBANS.

1339. HOURS OF OUR LADY. Manuscript on vellum, of late 15th century, Italian work, with illuminated borders and initials, and numerous miniatures. In certain of the prayers the name of "Loisius" is mentioned. This has been conjectured to be either Louis XII. of France or Louis de la Tremouille, Commander of the French forces in Italy. 8vo.

Lent by SAMUEL SANDARS, ESQ.

1340. THE STATUTES OF THE CITY OF PALERMO. Manuscript on vellum, of 15th century work, probably written at Palermo, with illuminated border and initials. Folio.

Lent by SAMUEL SANDARS, ESQ.

1341. THE HOURS OF OUR LADY OF ROMAN USE. Manuscript on vellum, of the 16th century, of Italian work, with beautiful miniatures and illuminations. On a page at the beginning are the arms of Antonio Landriani of Milan, for whom the book was probably executed. Small 4to.

Lent by THOMAS BROOKE, ESQ.

1342. STATUTES AND REGISTER OF THE GUILD OF THE TAVERNERS OF PERUGIA, beginning in 1379, and containing additional entries down to 1430. Manuscript on vellum. At the beginning of the volume is a large painting by Matteo di Ser Cambio. Small folio.

Lent by THOMAS BROOKE, ESQ.

1343. THE CONVIVIA SATURNALIA OF MACROBIUS. Manuscript on vellum, written at Rome by A. Tophius, and completed April 5th, 1466, with an illuminated title-page and initials. Folio.

Lent by SAMUEL SANDARS, ESQ.

1344. PSALTER, OF THE "VETUS ITALA" VERSION, WITH CANTICLES, CREEDS, LITANY, &c. Manuscript on vellum, written probably at Milan, in the 12th century, with illuminated initials, &c., in red and gold. Small 8vo.

Lent by THOMAS BROOKE, ESQ.

BALCONY.

PRINTED BOOKS.

LENT BY THE EARL OF CRAWFORD, K.T.

1345. LACTANTIUS, LUCIUS CÆCILIUS. Opera. De Divinis Institutionibus adversū gentes lib. vii.; De Ira Dei, &c. Editio princeps. Small folio. In Venerabili Monasterio Sublacensi, 1465, die vero 13 añpenultiā mensis Oct.

1346. AUGUSTINUS S., De Civitate Dei, libri xxii. lit. gotḥ. printed in double columns without title, numerals, catchwords, or signatures. (Ad fin.) Sub anno a nativitate domini M.CCCC.LXVII. Pontificat. Pauli Papae Secundi anno eius tertio. Tertio regnante Romanorum Imperatore Frederico indictione XV. die vero duodecima mensis Junii. Editio princeps. Large folio. (Subiaco. Sweynheym et Pannartz). 1467.

1347. LACTANTIUS, LUCIUS CÆCILIUS. Opera. Second edition of Lactantius. Folio. Romæ. In domo P. de Maximis per Con. Sweynheym et Arn. Pannartz, 1468.

1348. HIERONYMUS, SANCTUS. Epistolæ et Tractatus (cum prefationibus Joan. Andreæ, Epis. Aleriensis). Editio princeps. Two vols. Large folio. Rome. In domo Petri de Maximis (per Sweynheym et Pannartz), 1468. Vol. I. only is shown.

1349. CÆSAR, CAIUS JULIUS. Cæsaris Opera. Editio princeps. Folio. Romæ in domo Petri de Maximis, per Arn. Pannartz et Conr. Sweynheym, 12 May, 1469.

1350. LIVIUS PATAVINUS, TITUS. Historiarum Romanarum Decades III. (scil. Libr. 1-10 31, 32, 34-40) ex recognitione J. Andreæ Episc. Aleriensis. Three vols. Large folio. Rome. Sweynheym et Pannartz, S. A. (1469).

1351. CICERO. Opera Philosophica. Small folio. S. L. et A. (Rome. Ulric Hahn, 1469.) 32 lines to the page. S. L. et A.

According to Hain there should be a blank leaf after the 37th of the " De Officiis,' and another after the "Amicitia," but they are wanting in this copy. Printed in the smallest Roman type used by Ulric Hahn. Perhaps it should be called the Editio princeps.

1352. SUETONIUS, CAIUS TRANQUILLUS. Vitæ xii Cæsarum (ex recognitione Ant. Campani). Editio princeps. Folio. Absolutus Romæ in pinea regione via Pape anno a Christi natali 1470, sextili mēse.

35 lines to the page. Probably the first book printed by Philip de Lignamine. Printed in Roman letter, with the Greek passages in Greek characters. Sunderland copy.

1353. SALLUSTIUS, CRISPUS CAIUS. Bellum Catilinarium et Jugurthinum. Large 4to. Venetiis. Vindelin de Spira, 1470. Printed on vellum.

1354. JUSTINUS, M. JUNIUS. Historiæ ex Trogo Pompeio in epitomen redactæ et libris xliv. distinctæ. Editio princeps. Small folio. Venetiis. Per Nicolaum Jenson 1470.

1355. BIBLE (Latin). [The Bible, *Lat.*, Edited by J. Andreas.] *Begin.* [Vol. 1, fol. 2, recto.] Io. An[dreæ] Episcopi Alerieñ ad Paulum II. Venetum Pon. Max. epistola [verso]. Sequitur tabula, etc. [Fol. 2, verso]. Paulo II. Veneto summo Pont. Mathias Palmerius fœlicitate. [Line 30.] Aristeas ad Philocratem fratrem per Mathiam Palmeriũ Pisanũ e Grēco in Latinũ cõversus [Fol. 19, recto]. Incipit epistola sancti Hieronymi ad Paulinũ presbyterũ de omnibus divine historie libris [Fol. 22, recto, last line]. Incipit liber Bresith quem nos Genesin dicimus I. [*Fnd.*] Finis Psalterii. [Vol. 2, fol. 1, recto.] Epistola sācti Hieronymi p̄sbyteri ad Chromatiũ et Heliodorum Episcopos de Libris Salomonis [Colophon] Aspicis illustris lector quicunq̄ libellos/ Si cupis artificum nomina nosse : lege./ Aspera videbis cognomina Teutona : forsan/ Mitiget ars musis inscia uerba uirum./ Cõradus suueynheym : Arnoldus panartzq̄ magistri/ Rome impresserunt talia multa simul/ Petrus cum fratro Francisco Maximus ambo/ Huic operi aptatam contribuere domum/

M.CCCC.LXXI. [On the recto of the following leaf], (Incipiunt interpretationes Hebraicorum Nominum). 2 vols. Folio. Rome, Sweynheym and Pannartz, 1471.

Printed in long lines, Roman letter. 46 lines to the page, without any mark. Initials &c. illuminated. In the original oak boards. Vol. I. only is shown.

1356. EUTROPIUS. Incipit Eutropius historiographus et post eum Paulus Diaconus de historiis Italice Provincie ac Romanorum. Editio princeps. Folio. Impressus die lune xx. mensis Maii, 1471.

Printed by G. Laver. Sunderland copy.

1357. LACTANTIUS FIRMIANUS. De divinis institutionibus adversus gentes. Printed on vellum. Fol. s. l. (Venice.) Adam, 1471.

Nothing is known of this printer. Only one other vol. is known from his Press, the Virgil of the same year. It is the rarest of the Editions of Lactantius, and on vellum only one other copy is known, that in the Bibl. Nationale.

1358. ZOVENZONIUS, RAPHAEL. Carmen concitatorium. . . ad principes Christianos in Turcum. Small 4to. (Venice) Adam (de Ambergau, about 1471). (6) ff.

1359. NEPOS, CORNELIUS. Vitæ Virorum Excellentium. Editio princeps. 4to. Venetiis. Per Nicolaum Jenson impressum, viii idus Martias, 1471.

1360. PLINIUS, CAIUS SECUNDUS, JUNIOR. Epistolarum lib. viii. Editio princeps. Small folio. S. L. et Nom. Imp. 1471.

This edition is generally attributed to the press of Christ. Valdarfer, at Venice. Syston Park copy.

1361. PEROTTUS, NICOLAS. Liber de Metris . . . Epistola de generibus metrorum quibus Horatius Flaccus et S. Boetius usi sunt . . . 4to, Bologna, 1471.

Printed with the same type as the *Ovid* of Azzoguidi, and of the same date; this must be one of the earliest books printed in Bologna. For want of Greek type spaces are left. Dibdin (*Cassano Libr.*, Vol. II., p. 319) says of it, "Questionless, one of the rarest books in the world."

1362. POMPEIUS, FESTUS. De Significatione Verborum. Editio princeps. Large 4to. Mediolani (Ant. Zarothus), 1471.

L

One of the first books printed in Milan. The type is the same as that used by Zarotus in 1474 for his Liber Serapionis.   Sunderland copy.

1363. LYRA, NICOLAS DE. Postillæ Perpetuæ in Veteris et Novi Testamenti cum Epistola Jo. An. Aleriensis Episcopi ad Summum Pontificem. Five vols. Folio. Romæ. C. Sweynheym et A. Pannartz in Domo P. de Maximis, 1471-72.

Vol. I.—Dated 18 Nov. 1471. Vol. II.—Dated 26 Maii, 1472. Vol. III.—Dated 14 Januarii, 1472. Vol. IV.—No colophon or date. Vol. V.—13 Martii, 1472. 46 lines to the page, without any marks. The celebrated letter to the Pope Sextus IV., giving the catalogue of the works and the number of copies issued by this press, is found in this volume, which is the only one here shown.

1364. PRISCIANUS. (De Arte grammatica libri XVI.—De octo partibus orationis aliisque. —De præexercitamentis Rhetoricæ ex Hermogene, Ruffini Comment. de metris. —Dionysius de Situ Orbis, Prisciano interprete.) Folio. S.L. (Venice. Vindelin de Spira.) 1472.

The 2nd edition.   The Greek passages in Greek characters.   Old vellum.

1365. RUFFUS SEXTUS. De Historia Romana. De Ædificatione Venetiarum. Editio princeps. 4to. S L. et A. (Venice. Florentius de Argentina, circa 1472.) Sir M. M. Sykes' copy.

1366. VIRGILIUS MARO, P. Opera. Small folio. S. L. Leonardus Achates, 1472.

This book was probably printed at Vicenza, where it is known that Achates worked ; it has been wrongly ascribed to Basle and Venice, owing to the reading of the colophon.

1367. POLYBIUS. Polybii Historiæ, Latinè N. Perotto Interprete. Editio princeps of this version. Folio. Romæ. C. Sweynheym et A. Pannartz, die iouis ultima Decembris, 1473.

The last book printed by the two together, before the secession of Sweynheym to work at the engraving of the maps of the Ptolemy of 1478.

1368. XENOPHON. De Cyri Pædia lib. viii. a Fr. Philelpho Latinè versi. Editio princeps of this Latin edition. Small folio. (Romæ. Arnoldus de Villa, 1474.)

This is one of the copies in which only the date of the translation appears (at the foot of f. 145 verso). Sunderland copy.

1369. HERODOTUS. E Græco in Latinum habitæ per Laurentium Vallensem (ex recens. Bened. Brognoli). Editio princeps of this Latin version. Small folio. Venet. Impressus per Jacobum Rubeum, 1474. Heber copy.

1370. VALERIUS FLACCUS, CAIUS. Argonauticon lib. viii. Editio princeps. Small folio. Bononiæ. Impressum per Ugonem Rugerium et Dominum Bertochum, 1474, die 7 Maii. Sunderland copy.

1371. SENECA, L. A. Epistolæ. First edition with a date. Large 4to. Romæ. Arnold Pannartz, die I. mensis Feb., 1475.

It is printed in a peculiar semi-Gothic character, without marks. The Greek words are in Roman letter. Syston Park copy.

1372. TIBULLUS, ALBIUS. Carmina cum commentariis Bernardini (Cyllenii) Veronensis. Small 4to. Divided into two parts. Romæ. Anno 1475 die Mercurii 18. mensis Julii.

1373. AUGUSTINUS, S. De Civitate Dei, libri xxii. Folio. Venet. Gabriel Petri de Tarvisio, 1475.

1374. SENECA, L. A. Incipit lucii annei Senecæ cordubenis liber de moribus in quo nota-biliter et eleganter vitæ mores enarrat, &c. Editio princeps. Folio. Impressum hoc opus in civitate Neapolis, M [cccc] lxxiiiii. [1475].

This is one of the copies referred to by Brunet as having the six Latin verses beneath the colophon, and a list of contents after the register.

1375. PLINIUS, CAIUS SECUNDUS, JUNIOR. Epistolarum lib. ix. (ex. recog. Juniani Maii Parthenopei). Folio. Neapoli. Matt. Moravus, mense Julii, 1476.

The same type as that used for the Seneca, but more worn.

1376. BARTHOLOMEO DA LI SONNETTI, ZAMB. Isolario . . . Al Divo Cinquecento cinque e diece. Tre cinque ado Mil nulla tre e do un cèto nulla. questa opra dar piu cha altri lecce. 4to. S. L. et A. (circa 1477).

Verses on one side and maps on the other.
A rare geographical work, written in verse, and described by Dr. Dibdin as " one of the rarest volumes of early Italian poetry." The author gives his name on the fifth page.

1377. DIONYSIUS. De Situ Orbis habitabilis, ex versione Ant. Bechariæ, Lat. First edition of this version in prose. Small 4to. Impr. Venet. per Bern. Pictorem et Erharduin Ratdolt, 1477. Hamilton Palace, Beckford copy.

1378. PTOLOMÆUS, CLAUDIUS. Cosmographia (Latinè reddita, editionem curante Domitio Calderino). First edition with maps, forming also the first printed atlas. Folio. Rome. (Conrad Sweynheym et) Arnoldus Buckinck, vi Idus Octobris, 1478.

The letterings of the names are punched not engraved. The engraving of these maps was commenced by Conrad Sweynheym, when he retired from his association with Pannartz. The first leaf tells us that he was employed upon them for three years, after which he died ; and, that his work should not perish with him, it was taken up by Buckinck, who assumes all the credit in the colophon. It is commonly said that the Euclid of 1482 is the first book with mathematical figures, but we find here on ff. 9 and 10 woodcuts to illustrate the projection of the sphere used for the maps. It is the second book printed with copperplate engravings, the first being the '*Monte Sancto di Dio* of Bettini, in 1477.

1379. BERLINGHIERI, FRANCESCO. Geographia di Francesco Berlinghieri Fiorentino in terza rima et lingva toscana distincta con le sve tavole in varii siti et provincie secondo la geographia et distinctione dele tavole di Ptolomeo Cum gratia & Priuilegio :—Impresso in Firenze per Nicolo Todescho & emendato con somma diligentia dallo auctore. Large folio. S. L. et A. About 1478-1480.

1380. VITE de Sancti Padri. Folio. Venet. Nicolao Girardengo, 1479.

1381. VALERIUS MAXIMUS. Facta et Dicta Memorabilia. Folio. S. L. et A. (Brescia, Ferrandus.)

1382. JOSEPHUS GORIONIDES. Historia Judaica. Hebraicè. Editio princeps. Small folio. Mantua. Abraham Conath, S.A. (1480).

An abridgment of this history. A better edition appeared at Constantinople, 4to. 270 (1540).

1383. THEOCRITUS, SYRACUSANUS. Idyllia xviii. ; et Hesiodi Opera et Dies. Græc. Editio princeps. Small folio. S. L. et A.

30 lines to the page. From the similarity of its characters with the Lascaris, and the Greek Psalter printed at Milan in 1480-81, this work is attributed to the same press at the same date. See the interesting note of Ebert, vol. iv. p. 1870. Syston Park copy.

1384. APOLLONIUS, PETR. COLATINUS. De Eversione Urbis Ierusalem Heroicum Carmen Editio princeps. 4to. Milan. Uld. Scinczenzeller et Leonardus Pachel. xv. Kal. Nov. 1481.

Roman letter, 26 lines to the page. So rare, that in 1540 it was printed as an editio princeps at Paris by Jean de Gaigny. Syston Park copy.

1385. EUCLIDES. Elementorum lib. xv. a Græc. in Lat. translati cum commentariis Jo. Campani, lit. gotþ. With diagrams in the margins. Folio. Venet. Er. Ratdolt, June 8, 1482.

The most ancient edition of this version, and one of the first printed books in which mathematical figures occur (but *see* "Ptolemy," Ed. 1478, No. 1378).

1386. MASUCCIO, GUARDATO. Il Novellino con le .L. Argomenti & morali conclusiŏ . . . emědatum & correctum cum magna diligentia . . . Fol. Milan. Christophoro Waldatser (*sic*) 28th May 1483.

1387. STATIUS, PUBLIUS PAPINIUS. Opera ; id est Thebais cum interpretatione Placidi Lactantii ; Achilleis, cum recollectis traditis a Francisco Maturantio ; Sylvarum lib. v. cum commentario Dom. Calderini. Editio princeps of the complete works. Folio. Venetiis. Per Oct. Scotum, quarto nonas Decembris, 1483.

1388. PLATO. Opera. Latinè, interprete Marsilio Ficino. Two vols. in one. Editio princeps of this version and also the first publication of Plato in any language ; the earliest issue, before the leaves of errata were printed, and also before the impression of the preliminary matter. Small folio. Florence. Laurentius Venetus, s A. (1483—84). With Pirckheimer's book plate.

1389. PROBUS, VALERIUS. De Litteris Antiquis Opusculum. Editio princeps. Small 4to. s. l. (sed Bresciæ). Boninus de Boninis, 1486. Fazakerley woodcuts.

1390. HOMER. Batrachomyomachia, cum glossis interlinearibus characteribus rubris distinctus. Small 4to. Venet. Laonicus Cretensis, 1486.

A very rare and curious edition, printed in red and black in alternate lines, 28 lines to a page. Syston Park copy. Vellum.

1391. SCRIPTORES Veteres de re Militari scilicet ; Vegetius, Frontinus, Modestus, Ælianus. Editio princeps. Small 4to. Romæ per Eucharium Silber, 1487.

The first edition of each of these pieces, excepting the "Vegetius." Sunderland copy.

1392. ANTHOLOGIA. Epigrammatum Græcorum Planudis Rhet. Græc., cura Jo. Lascaris. Editio princeps, printed throughout in capital letters. 4to. Impressum Florent. per L. Franc. de Alopa, 1494.

Didot copy. Very fine old red mor. binding, inlaid with other coloured leather, by J. Lehner, of Vienna.

1393. MUSÆUS. Opusculum de Herone et Leandro quod et in Latinam linguam ad verbum tralatum est. Græc. et Lat. Small 4to. Venetiis. Aldus, circa 1494.

Generally regarded as the First Edition, and the first production of the Aldine press. There are two woodcuts in the text. Yemeniz copy.

1394. APOLLONIUS RHODIUS. Apollonii Rhodii Argonautica, cum Scholiis Græc. With text printed in capital letters : initial letters, and floriated borders illuminated in gold. Editio princeps. 4to. Florentiæ. (F. de Alopa) 1496. The La Vallière copy.

1395. HIERONYMO, SANCTO. Vita e Pistole Volgare (dal Frate Matteo da Ferrara Gesuato). Folio. Ferrara, Lorenzo di Rossi da Valenza, 1497.

Wanting the Vita, which is not mentioned in the Registro. Girardot de Préfond's copy.

1396. APICIUS, CŒLIUS. Apicius in Re Quoqinaria. Small 4to. Impress. Mediol. per Guill. Signerre, die 20 mensis Januarii, 1498.

First edition with a date. Title, as above, beneath which is the woodcut device of printer. Beckford copy.

1397. CICERO, MARCUS TULLIUS. Ciceronis Opera. Four volumes bound in two. Large folio. Mediolani. Per Alex. Minutianum et Guielmos fratres, 1498–99. Sunderland copy. Vols. I., II., are shown.

1398. ETYMOLOGICON MAGNUM GRÆCUM. Græc. (cum Græc. prefatione M. Musuri). Editio princeps. Large folio. Venet. Sumpt. Nic. Blasti opera Zach. Calliergi, 1499. Illuminated with the arms of the Medici.

1399. EURIPIDES. Tragoediae iv. Medea, Hippolytus, Alcestis et Andromache. Græc. cura Jo. Lascaris. Editio princeps of the four plays. Small 4to. S. L. et A. (Florent. Per Laurent, Fran. de Alopa, ante 1500.) This copy is of the revised issue, with the 12 leaves reprinted. Vellum.

COLLECTION OF BOOKS LENT BY CAPTAIN G. L. HOLFORD, C.I.E.

1400. THE DIVINA COMEDIA OF DANTE ALIGHIERI. Printed at Foligno by Joannes Neumeister, 1472. The first edition.

1401. THE GREEK GRAMMAR OF CONSTANTINE LASCARIS, edited by Demetrius Cretensis. Printed at Milan by Dionisio Paravisini, 1476. First edition of the first book printed in Greek characters.

1402. HOMER. Printed at Florence by Demetrias Chalcondylas for Bernardus and Nerius Nerlii, 1488. The first edition. 2 vols, in original Venetian stamped leather binding.

1403. "HYPNEROTOMACHIA POLIPHILI," by Francesco Colonna. Printed at Venice by Aldus Manutius, for Leonardo Craseo of Verona, 1499. "One of the most famous books in the annals of Venetian printing." With many woodcuts. On Vellum.

1404. Θησέος καὶ Γάμοι τῆς Ἐμηλιᾶς. A translation into modern Greek of Boccacio's Teseide. Printed at Venice by Giovanantonio et fratelli da Sabbio, 1529. With many wood-cuts of the school of Zoan Andrea and others.

1405. THE DIVINA COMEDIA OF DANTE ALIGHIERI, with the commentary of Martino Paolo Nidobeato and Guido Terzago. Printed at Milan by Lud. and Alber. Pedimontani, 1478. Folio.

1406. THE DIVINA COMEDIA OF DANTE ALIGHIERI, with the commentary of Christoforo Landini. Printed at Florence by Nicolaus Lorenz of Breslau, 1481. With illustrations on copper, probably by Baccio Baldini from designs of Botticelli. Folio.

1407. THE DIVINA COMEDIA OF DANTE ALIGHIERI, with the life by Boccaccio and the commentary of Christofal Berardus. Printed at Venice by Windelin of Spires, 1477. 4to.

1408. "PUBLII OVIDII NASONIS HEROIDUM EPISTOLÆ, ETC." Printed at Venice by Aldus Manutius, 1502. The first Aldine edition of Ovid. 8vo.

1409. "HORATIUS." Printed at Venice by Aldus Manutius, 1501. The first Aldine edition. 8vo.

1410. "VERGILIUS." Printed at Venice by Aldus Manutius, 1501. The first Aldine edition. 8vo.

1411. "MARTIALIS." Printed at Venice by Aldus Manutius, 1501. The first Aldine edition. On vellum. 8vo.

1412. "BIBLIA SACRA." Printed at Venice by Nicolaus Jenson, 1479. On vellum, with an illuminated border to the first page of Genesis, and an illuminated title-page, both bearing the arms of Della Rovere. This copy is said to have belonged to Pope Sixtus IV. Folio.

1413. THE WORKS OF HORACE. Printed at Milan by Philippus de Lavagnia, 1476. Folio.

1414. Ὁμήρου Ἰλιὰς μεταβληθεῖσα πάλαι εἰς κοινὴν γλῶσσαν νῦν δὲ διορθωθεῖσα . . . παρὰ Νικολάου τοῦ Λουκάνου. A translation into modern Greek verse of the Iliad of Homer, by Nicolaus Lucanus. Printed at Venice by Stefano da Sabio, 1526. With many woodcuts. 4to.

1415. THE "EPISTOLÆ AD ATTICUM, BRUTUM ET QUINTUM FRATREM" OF CICERO. Printed at Venice by Nicolaus Jenson, 1470. With an illuminated border. Folio.

1416. Ὁμήρου Ἰλιάς. HOMERI ILIAS. Printed at Venice by Lucantonio Giunta, 1537. 8vo.

1417. "LE TERZE RIME DI DANTE." Printed at Venice by Aldus Manutius, 1502. The first Aldine edition. 8vo.

1418. "VALTURIUS DE RE MILITARI." Printed at Verona by Joannes de Verona, 1472. The first book printed at Verona, and the first *dated* book with woodcuts executed in Italy. Folio.

1419. "OPERE VOLGARI DI MESSER FRANCESCO PETRARCHA." Printed at Fano by Hieronimo Soncino, 1503. 8vo.

1420. ÆSOP'S FABLES in Greek and Latin. Printed at Milan by Bonus Accursius in 1480. The first edition of the first Greek classic printed. 4to.

1421. THE "PHILOCOLO" OF GIOVANNI BOCCACCIO. Printed at Naples by Sixtus Reissinger, 1478. With several large woodcuts. 4to.

1422. "MAURI SERVII HONORATI GRAMMATICI IN TRIA VIRGILII OPERA EXPOSITIO." Printed at Rome by Udalricus Gallus [Ulric Hahn], 1472. With a curious punning colophon, probably by Campanus. One of the earliest books in which Greek characters were printed. Folio.

1423. "LE COSE VOLGARI DI MESSER FRANCESCO PETRARCHA." Printed at Venice by Aldus Manutius, 1501. The first Aldine edition. 8vo.

1424. "LE COSE VOLGARI DE MESSER FRANCESCO PETRARCHA." The first Lyons counterfeit of the Aldine Petrarch. Printed *circ.* 1501. 8vo.

1424a. "ALIQUI LIBRI EX ILIADE HOMERI TRANSLATI PER DOMINUM NICOLAUM DE VALLE." Printed at Rome, by Joannes Philippus de Lignamine, 1474. 4to.

1424b. "MONTE SANCTO DI DIO COMPOSTO DA MESSER ANTONIO [BETTINI] DA SIENA. VESCHOVO DI FOLIGNO." Printed at Florence by Nicolaus Lorenz, 1477. With three plates on copper.

1424c. ÆSOP'S FABLES, IN LATIN AND ITALIAN, edited by Francesco Tuppo. Printed at Naples, probably by Matthias Moravus of Olmütz, 1485. With many large woodcuts and ornamental borders. 4to.

1425. "LEPISTOLE DOUIDIO NASONE DI CAMPAGNA." The Epistles of Ovid, "translatate di gramaticha in uolgare fiorentino." Printed at Naples by Sixtus Riessinger, *circ.* 1475. With many coloured woodcuts.

Lent by C. FAIRFAX MURRAY, ESQ.

1426. "MEDITATIONES ... JOHANNIS DE TURRECREMATA ... CARDINALIS." Printed at Rome by Ulric Hahn, called in the book "Udalricus Gallus," 1473. The first illustrated edition of these meditations was printed by Hahn in 1467 and is the first book in which woodcuts were used in Italy. The same blocks were used in this edition, and in that of 1478, and "illustrate the same subjects as the frescoes recently painted by the Cardinal's order in the Church of Santa Maria sopra Minerva at Rome" Small folio.

Lent by SAMUEL SANDARS, ESQ.

1427. "MEDITATIONES ... JOHANNIS DE TURRECREMATA ... CARDINALIS." Printed at Rome by Ulric Hahn, called in this book "Udalricus Gallus," 1478. With many large woodcuts.
Lent by WILLIAM MORRIS, ESQ.

1428. "MEDITATIONES ... JOHANNIS DE TURRECREMATA." Printed by Johannes Neumeister, 1479 This book, generally considered to have been printed at Foligno, appears by the type and general work to have been printed at Mayence. Another edition, with the same woodcuts, was printed by Neumeister, with French type, at Albi in 1481. This copy is in the original German binding.
Lent by WILLIAM MORRIS, ESQ.

1429. "MEDITATIONES ... JOANNIS DA TURRECREMATA." Printed at Rome by Stephen Planrck, 1498. With many woodcuts.
Lent by WILLIAM MORRIS, ESQ.

1430. "OFFICIA BEATE MARIE SECUNDUM USUM ROMANE ECCLESIE." The Hours of Our Lady. Printed at Venice by Joannes Hamman "dictus Hertzog," MDCCCCXCXIII. [1503]. With engraved border to every page, and many pictures.
Lent by C. FAIRFAX MURRAY, ESQ

1431. "SECUNDUS DYALOGORUM LIBER BEATI GREGORII PAPE DE VITA AC MIRACULIS BEATISSIMI BENEDICTI." St. Gregory's Life of St. Benedict, followed by the Rule of St. Benedict, and the "Speculum Bernardi Abbatis Casinensis de his adque in professione obligatur monachus." Printed at Venice by Lucantonio Giunta, 1505.
Lent by C. FAIRFAX MURRAY, ESQ.

1432. "MIRABILIA ROMÆ." A description of the antiquities, churches, &c, of Rome, for the use of pilgrims. Printed at Rome by Stephen Plannck, 1499. With many woodcuts.
Lent by C. FAIRFAX MURRAY, ESQ.

1433. "MIRABILIA ROMÆ." Another edition of the same, printed at Rome by Eucharius Silber, 1505. Bound up with other small tracts printed for pilgrims.
Lent by C. FAIRFAX MURRAY, ESQ.

1434 " HEC SUNT QUINDECIM COLLECTE SIVE ORATIONES . . . B[EA]TE BIRGITTE." The
fifteen prayers of St. Bridget, followed by a prayer of St. Augustine. Without
place or date. Printed at Rome by Stephen Planck, *circ.* 1500. With a woodcut.
Lent by C. FAIRFAX MURRAY, ESQ.

1435. " CONJURATIONES DEMONUM." Exorcisms of evil spirits "in corporibus hominum
existentium." Without place or date. Printed at Rome by Stephen Plannck,
circ. 1500. With a woodcut.
Lent by C. FAIRFAX MURRAY, ESQ.

1436. THE RULE OF ST. BENEDICT. Printed at Venice by Bernardino Benalio, 1489.
" S[e]c[un]d[u]s lib[er] Dyalogorum beati Gregorii pape de vita et miraculis . . .
Benedicti abbatis." Printed by the same, 1489. With woodcuts.
Lent by C. FAIRFAX MURRAY, ESQ.

1437. " TRANSLATIO MIRACULOSA ECCLESIE BEATE MARIE VIRGINIS DE LORETO." An
account of the translation of the Holy House to Loreto. Without place or date.
Printed at Rome by Stephen Plannck, *circ.* 1500. With a woodcut.
Lent by C. FAIRFAX MURRAY, ESQ.

1438. " QUATRIREGIO DEL DECORSO DELLA VITA HUMANA." A poem by Federico Frezzi,
Bishop of Foligno. Printed at Florence, "Ad petitione di Ser Piero Pacini da
Pescia, 1508." With many woodcuts. The first illustrated edition. Folio.
Lent by SIR EDWARD BURNE-JONES, BART.

1439. " ORDO MISSALIS S[E]C[UN]D[U]M CONSUETUDINE[M] ROMANE CURIE." Printed at
Rome by Stephen Plannck, 1496. On vellum, with coloured woodcuts, a richly
illuminated border to the first page of the missal, and a fine miniature of the
Crucifixion before the Canon. Folio.
Lent by THOMAS BROOKE, ESQ.

1440. " MISSALE MO[N]ASTICU[M] S[ECUNDU]M C[ON]SUETUDINE[M] ORDINIS VALLISUM-
- BROSE." Printed at Venice by Lucantonio Giunta, 1503. On vellum. With
many woodcuts. Folio.
Lent by THOMAS BROOKE, ESQ.

1441. " OFFICIOLUM BEATE MARIE VIRGINIS S[ECUNDU]M C[ON]SUETUDINEM ROMANE
CURIE." Printed at Venice by Lucantonio Giunta, 1503. On vellum. With
woodcuts. Very small 32mo.
Lent by THOMAS BROOKE, ESQ.

1442. "OFFICIUM BEATE MARIE S[ECUNDU]M USUM ROMANU[M]." Printed at Venice by Lucantonio Giunta, 1505. On vellum. With woodcuts. 8vo.

Lent by THOMAS BROOKE, ESQ.

1443. "HISTORIA DE VITA ET GESTIS SCANDERBEGI EPIROTARUM PRINCIPIS." By Marinus Barletius. Printed at Rome by B.V., *i.e.* Bernardus Venetus de Vitalibus, *circ.* 1508. With a portrait of Scanderbeg. First edition. Folio.

Lent by MESSRS. ELLIS AND ELVEY.

1444. "EPISTOLE ET EVANGELII, ET LETIONI VOLGARI IN LINGUA THOSCANA, NUOVAMENTE RISTAMPATE." The Epistles and Gospels in Italian, printed at Florence by the Giunti, 1551. With beautiful woodcuts and frontispiece, which appear also in three earlier editions.

Lent by WILLIAM MORRIS, ESQ.

1445. "NINFALE FIESOLANO DI M. GIOVANNI BOCCACCIO." Printed at Florence by Valente Panizzi, 1568. With eighteen woodcuts of the 15th century taken from an earlier edition. 4to.

Lent by R. C. FISHER, ESQ.

1446. "PROTESTO FACTO ALLA SIGNORIA DI FIRENZE ET A TUCTI GLI ALTRI MAGISTRATI PER CONSERVARE LA LIBERTA & MANTENERE LA JUSTITIA." By Francesco di Nicolo Berlinghieri. A discourse pronounced on January 15th, 1477. Printed at Florence, *circ.* 1490. With a woodcut. 8vo.

Lent by R. C. FISHER, ESQ.

1447. "PHILIPPI CALANDRI AD . . . JULIANUM LAURENTII MEDICÉ DE ARIMETHRICA OPUSCULU[M]." Printed at Florence by Lorenzo de Morgiani and Giovanni Thedesco da Maganza [Johann Petri of Mayence], 1491. The first printed book on arithmetic. With a number of curious woodcuts illustrating the problems. Small 4to.

Lent by R. C. FISHER, ESQ.

1448. THE RULE OF ST. BENEDICT, with the Exposition of Cardinal de Turrecremata, the Rule of the Congregation of St. Justine of Padua, and the Rules of SS. Basil and Augustine. Printed at Venice by Lucantonio Giunta, 1500. With woodcuts and ornamented borders. 4to.

Lent by R. C. FISHER, ESQ.

1449. "ARTE DEL BEN MORIRE CIOE IGRATIA DI DIO . . . COMPOSTO PER . . . MON-
SIGNOR CARDINALE DI FERMO [DOMENICO CAPRANICA]." Printed at Florence
circ. 1500. With many woodcuts. The only copy known. Small 4to.

Lent by R. C. FISHER, ESQ.

1450. "LE DIVOTE MEDITATIONE SOPRA LA PASSIONE DEL NOSTRO SIGNORE CHAVATE
& FONDATE ORIGINALMENTE SOPRA SANCTO BONAVENTURA . . . SOPRA
NICOLAO DE LIRA." Printed at Florence, *circ.* 1490. With many woodcuts.
Small 4to.

Lent by R. C. FISHER, ESQ.

1451. "LIBRO DELLA VITA MONASTICA," by Lorenzo Giustiniani, Patriarch of Venice.
Printed at Venice in 1494. With a woodcut portrait of the author preceded by
his cross-bearer, and two emblematic devices. Small 4to.

Lent by R. C. FISHER, ESQ.

1451a. "ARTE DEL BEN MORIRE CIOE IGRATIA DI DIO." By Domenico Capranica.
Printed at Florence, 1513. With the same woodcuts as the earlier edition (see
No. 1449). 4to.

Lent by C. FAIRFAX MURRAY, ESQ.

1451b. "LE DIVOTE MEDITATIONE SOPRA LA PASSIONE DEL NOSTRA SIGNORE." By St.
Bonaventura. Printed at Venice by "Matheo di Co de cha," 1489. With many
woodcuts. Small 4to.

Lent by C. FAIRFAX MURRAY, ESQ.

1451c. "CORIOLANI CEPIONIS DALMATÆ PETRI MOCENICI IMPERATORIS [*i.e.* DOGE OF
VENICE] GESTORUM LIBER." Printed at Venice by Bernardus Pictor, Erhardus
Ratdolt, and Petrus Loslein, 1477. With a woodcut border to the first page.
Small 4to.

Lent by C. FAIRFAX MURRAY, ESQ.

1451d. "ARTE DI BEN MORIRE." By Domenico Capranica. Printed at Venice either by
Ratdolt or Renner of Hailbrun, 1478. With a woodcut border of oak-leaves.
Small 4to.

Lent by C. FAIRFAX MURRAY, ESQ.

1451*e*. "KALENDARIO." An astronomical calendar with diagram, tables, &c. Printed at Venice by Bernardus Pictor, Petrus Loslein, and Erhardus Ratdolt, 1476. The first book with an ornamental title-page. In the original wooden boards. Small folio.

Lent by C. FAIRFAX MURRAY, ESQ.

1451*f*. "MISSALE AD USUM CHORI ECCLESIE SARUM ANGLICANE." Printed at Venice by Johannes Hertzog de Landoia, 1494. Hertzog printed another and smaller edition of the Salisbury Missal. With woodcut borders. Folio.

Lent by SAMUEL SANDARS, ESQ.

1451*g*. "M. ANTONII COCCII SABELLICI RERUM VENETARUM AB URBE CONDITA IN UNIVERSUM OPUS." Printed at Venice by Andreas de Toresanis de Asula, 1487. With illuminated initials, &c. Folio.

Lent by SAMUEL SANDARS, ESQ.

1451*h*. "OFFICIUM BEATE MARIE VIRGINIS SECUNDUM CONSUETUDINEM ROMANE CURIE." Printed at Venice by Johannes Emericus of Spires, 1498. With woodcuts. 16mo. Lent by SAMUEL SANDARS, ESQ.

1451*i*. ÆSOP'S FABLES IN LATIN AND ITALIAN. Edited by Francesco Tuppo. Printed at Aquila by Eusanius de Stella, Joannes Picardus de Hamell, and Loisius de Masson, 1493. The woodcuts are copied from those in the Naples edition of 1485.

Lent by SAMUEL SANDARS, ESQ.

1452. "OPERA NOVA CONTEMPLATIVA P[ER] OGNI FIDEL CHRISTIANO." A block-book containing pictures representing Old Testament types and prophecies with the corresponding New Testament antitypes and fulfilments. Printed at Venice by Giovani Andrea Vavassore detto Vadagni, *circ.* 1510. 8vo.

Lent by SAMUEL SANDARS, ESQ.

1452*a*. "LIBRO DI FRATE HIERONYMO DA FERRARA (SAVONAROLA). DELLA SIMPLICITA DELLA VITA CHRISTIANA. TRADOCTO IN VOLGARE." Printed by Lorenzo Morgiani, at Florence, 1496.

Lent by the RIGHT REV. THE BISHOP OF PORTSMOUTH.

1452*b*. "GRAMMATICA HEBRAICÆ LINGUÆ" By Agathius Guidacer. Printed at Rome, 1514. First Edition.

Lent by the RIGHT REV. THE BISHOP OF PORTSMOUTH.

COLLECTION OF AUTOGRAPH LETTERS. LENT BY ALFRED MORRISON, ESQ.

1453. BENVENUTO CELLINI to Vincenzo Borghini, Prior of the Innocents at Florence, dated di casa, 13 April, 1564. Excusing himself from attending the obsequies of Michelangelo on the plea of ill-health. *Holograph.*

1454. FRA SEBASTIANO LUCIANO, called Sebastiano del Piombo. Document dated. Roma, 23 May, 1543. *Holograph.*

1455. LIONARDO DA VINCI. Two pen-and-ink sketches of machines, undated. (It will be observed that the sketches are described in inversed characters, a practice adopted by the painter to prevent his inventions being divulged by his servants.)

1456. PIETRO VANUCCI, called "Perugino" to Isabella d'Este, Duchess of Mantua. Undated (16 August, 1504). He is working at the Duchess's picture, and with God's help hopes to finish it shortly. *Holograph.*

1457. RAFFAELE SANTI, called "Raphael Sanzio." Document dated Rome, 1 January, 1515. A receipt for 200 ducats for two months' work on the paintings at the Vatican. *In Latin with autograph signature.*

1458. GIORGIO VASARI to Giovanni Caccini. Dated Florence, 6 December, 1562. He is looking forward to paying Caccini a visit, but he has been and still is ill. *Holograph.*

1459. GIULIO PIPPI, called "Romano," to the deputies of the manufactory of Steccata. Dated Mantua, 30 April, 1541. Regretting his absence when Michelangelo called for the drawing. He is quite ready to go to Parma to paint frescoes if his patron will give permission. *Holograph.*

1460. ANDREA DORIA, Admiral, to the Protectors of the Bank of St. George. Dated "Dalla mia Galea Capit. sopra San Firenze," 21 February, 1554. *Autograph Signature.*

1461. PIETRO, CARDINAL BEMBO, letter dated Padua, 11 September, 1539. *Holograph.*

1462. POPE CLEMENT VII. [Guilio de' Medici] to the Emperor Charles V. Dated Rome, 28 September, 1529. *Holograph.*

1463 POPE JULIUS II. (Giuliano della Rovere) to Bianca Maria Sforza, Duchess of Milan. Dated Rome, 16 June, 1478. *Holograph.*

1464. POPE JULIUS III. (Gianmaria del Monte) to Henry II., King of France. Dated " Ex Palatio nostro apostolico," 4 July, 1550. *Holograph.*

1465. EMERICO VESPUCCI (the famous navigator, from whom America received its name) to his father. Dated Trivio Mugelli, 18 October, 1476. He apologises for writing in Latin, for his knowledge of that language is not very great. There is no news except that everybody wants to move and live near the city. *Holograph.*

1466. POPE PIUS IV. (Gianangelo de' Medici) to Cardinal de Neocastro. Dated Rome, 27 April, 1540. *Holograph.*

1467. BALDASSARE, COUNT CASTIGLIONE, to Frederick di Gonzaga, Marquis of Mantua. Dated Rome, 1 January, 1521. He hears that a follower of Cardinal Colonna has a portrait of the Marquis, painted by Raphael, and he doubts not that the Cardinal will succeed in securing it, and will present it to his correspondent. *Holograph.*

1468. PIETRO ARETINO to Cosimo de' Medici. Dated Venice, 28 October, 1547. He protests that he never had any intercourse with the exiles, and supposes that the Duke intends to give him pecuniary assistance, of which he is in much need. *Holograph.*

1469. LUCREZIA BORGIA, Duchess of Ferrara, to the poet Antonio Tebaldeo; credentials of Hectore Beringero. Dated Rome, 20 November, 1501. *Autograph signature.*

1470. BONIFAZIO BEMBO to the Duke of Milan, announcing that he had finished the work which the Duke had given him in "la salla del Castello de Pavia," and had come to wait for further orders. Dated " In Modoetia," 15 August, 1468. *Holograph.* Signed " Bonifacius da Cremona pi:tor."

1471. PROSPERO COLONNA to the Duke of Milan.   Dated "Romanenghi," 4 March, 1514. *Autograph signature.*

1472. FRANCESCO FILELFO, called Philelphus, "miles et poeta laureatus," " Illustrissimo Principi nostro Moguntie " (the Archbishop Elector of Mayence).   Undated (*circ.* 1450). *Holograph.*

1473. ANTONIO BALLISTO DI SAN GALLO to Piero Soderini.   Dated 6 February, 1508. On the subject of the work he was then carrying on at the Castle of St. Angelo. *Holograph.*

1474. GIOVANNI PICO DELLA MIRANDOLA, called the " Phœnix of Wits," to his nephew. Dated Ferrara, 15 May, 1492. A letter of pious exhortation. (A translation of it by Sir Thomas More is published in Mirandola's Life.) *Holograph in Latin.*

1475. COSIMO DE' MEDICI, called "The Father of his Country," to Francesco Sforza Duke of Milan. Dated Florence, 11 March, 1453. *Holograph.*

1476. LORENZO DE' MEDICI, called " Il Magnifico," to the Duke of Milan.   Dated Florence, 15 January, 1480. *Holograph.*

1477. PIERO II. DE' MEDICI to Dionigi de' Pucci, " Oratori Florentino."   Dated Florence, 13 February, 1473. Expressing many obligations to the king. *Holograph.*

1478. GIULIANO I. DE' MEDICI to his brother Lorenzo.   Dated 22 January, 1473. *Holograph.*

1479. POPE LEO X. (Giovanni de' Medici), the restorer of learning, to Charles VIII. King of France. Dated 2 April, 1493. In Latin. He has often acknowledged his correspondent's kindness to him and his brothers, a kindness which deserves every return, for it makes them feel that they have not lost a father. Dangers which as far as regards themselves they would avoid they will always be willing to incur at the King's bidding. *Holograph.*

1480. GIOVANNI DE' MEDICI, called "delle Bande Nere." Document dated Padua, 16 June, 1525. *Autograph signature.*

1481. GIULIANO II. DE' MEDICI to the office of St. George. Dated Rome, 19 April, 1515. Respecting a vessel laden with salt, belonging to a friend of his, which has put into Porto Venere. He entreats the office not to put any obstacle in the way of its free sailing. *Autograph signature.*

1482. GUIDO, CARDINAL DE' MEDICI, to Roberto de' Beccutis. Dated Rome, 7 April, 1522. On financial matters. *Holograph.*

1483. COSIMO DE' MEDICI (first Grand Duke of Tuscany) to Signor Geraldi (then residing in London). Dated 28 August, 1544. Referring to money matters between the writer and the King of England, which are being conducted by Antonio Giudotti. *Autograph signature.*

1484. ANGELO AMBROGINI, called "Poliziano," to Lorenzo de' Medici. Dated Pisa, 20 September, 1478. He believes his letters must be interesting to his correspondent because he always writes about the latter's relations. *Holograph.*

1485. AMBROGIO FOPPA (called "Caradosso") to Lodovico Maria Sforza, Duke of Milan. Dated Rome, 25 February, 1495. He has seen the Cardinal of Parma, who, on his telling him he had come to Rome in search of antique marbles and bronzes, informed him that he had a statue which he should be happy to offer to 'the Duke. *Holograph.*

1486. GALEAZZO MARIA SFORZA to his father. Dated Veileppano, 30 January, 1466. In favour of a friend of his, Filippo da Gallara, to whom he hopes his father will see justice done. *Autograph signature.*

1487. BORSO D'ESTE, Duke of Ferrara, to Francesco Sforza, Duke of Milan. Dated Ferrara, 27 May, 1455. *Holograph.*

1488. IPPOLITA MARIA SFORZA, Queen of Naples, to the Ambassador Lanfredi. Dated Pucheolis, 15 October, 1486. On the subject of the Priory of Capua, for which she understands the Countess Camerlenga is applying on behalf of one of her sons. *Holograph.*

1489. GIOVANNI GALEAZZO MARIA SFORZA to Alessandro Proveno. Dated Milan, December 28, 1483. *Autograph signature.*

1490. FRANCESCO MARIA SFORZA, Duke of Milan, to the office of St. George. Dated Milan, 17 June, 1522. Accrediting his nuncio, Roberto Archinto, as a person to be thoroughly trusted. *In Latin, with autograph signature.*

1491. ISABELLA OF ARAGON, Duchess of Milan, wife of Giovanni Galeazzo Sforza, to the Emperor Charles V. Dated Naples, 18 February, 1521. A letter of congratulation on his coronation. *Holograph.*

1492. JOANNA OF ARAGON, Princess Colonna of Tagliacozzi, to Piero de' Medici. A complimentary letter. Dated Roma, 5 October, 1572. *Autograph conclusion and signature.* Her portrait by Raphael is in the Louvre.

1493. MASSIMILIANO MARIA SFORZA, Duke of Milan, to Lodovico Visconti. Dated Verona, 4 November, 1512. Discrediting Hieronymo da Carbrono, who has been sent on a mission without his knowledge. *Autograph signature.*

1494. LODOVICO MARIA SFORZA, Duke of Milan. Dated 24 July, 1490. He will do everything to bring the disturbance, of which his correspondent complains, to a speedy end. *Holograph in Latin.*

1495. CATARINA SFORZA, Countess of Riario (one of the most celebrated women of her time), to Lodovico Maria Sforza. Dated Forlini, 6 June, 1497. She is writing to Joanna Taverna about certain letters which she has been expecting from her correspondent, but which have not yet arrived. *Holograph.*

1496. FRANCESCO GUICCIARDINI. Letter dated 17 February, 1502. *Holograph.*

DRAWINGS.

LENT BY HER MAJESTY THE QUEEN.

1497. THE FLAGELLATION.

Illuminated page from a book formerly belonging to the Scalzi at Florence ; members of which fraternity are kneeling in supplication at the base of the column. Florentine. 14th century.

1498. HEAD OF AN OLD MAN.

By LORENZO DI CREDI.

1499. SKETCH BY ANDREA DEL SARTO FOR HIS MONOCHROME FRESCO OF THE BAPTISM OF ST. JOHN THE BAPTIST IN THE CLOISTERS OF THE SCALZO, FLORENCE.

1500. STUDY OF A FEMALE HEAD

By PERUGINO (?).

1501. THE ANNUNCIATION.

By FRA BARTOLOMMEO.

1502. MAN WRITING, AND SLEEPING DOG.

By MASACCIO.

1503. TWO STUDIES FOR THE VIRGIN WITH THE INFANT SAVIOUR ADORED BY ANGELS AND SAINTS.

By FRA BARTOLOMMEO.

1504. STUDY FOR THE FRESCO IN. THE SISTINE CHAPEL AT THE VATICAN OF THE CHARGE TO ST. PETER.

By PERUGINO.

1505. TWO STUDIES FOR THE HOLY FAMILY.

By FRA BARTOLOMMEO.

1506. Studies of Figures.
By Lionardo da Vinci.

1507. Seven Studies of Figures.
By Lionardo da Vinci.

1508. Studies for the Heads of Homer, Virgil, and Dante.
From the Fresco of Parnassus in the Stanza of the Vatican.
By Raphael.

1509. Sketch for the Cartoon of the Miraculous Draught
of Fishes.
By Raphael.

1510. The Fall of Phaeton.
By Michelangelo.

1511. Academical Study of the Proportions of the Nude
Figure.
By Michelangelo.

1512. Three of the Labours of Hercules.
By Michelangelo.

1513. Studies of Plants.
By Lionardo da Vinci.

1514. Pen and Ink Sketch.
From the Fresco in the |Loggia of the Vatican, of the dividing of the land by lot
before Moses and Aaron.
By Raphael.

1515. Studies of Plants and Flowers.
By Lionardo da Vinci.

1516. STUDY OF A FEMALE HEAD. In Silver Point.
By LIONARDO DA VINCI.

1517. FOUR ACADEMICAL STUDIES OF THE NUDE MALE FIGURE.
By LIONARDO DA VINCI.

1518. STUDIES OF TREES.
By LIONARDO DA VINCI.

1519. STUDIES OF HANDS.
By LIONARDO DA VINCI.

1520. FEMALE HEADS WITH ELABORATELY PLAITED HAIR.
This type of head was copied by Giov. Bazzi in his picture of Leda.
By LIONARDO DA VINCI.

1521. STUDIES OF HEADS. In Silver Point on blue paper.

By LIONARDO DA VINCI.

1522. STUDY OF A HEAD.
By FILIPPINO LIPPI.

1523. STUDIES OF FIGURES, DRAPERY, &C.
The feet are studies for the Holy Family in the Louvre.
By LIONARDO DA VINCI.

1524. THE BETRAYAL OF CHRIST.
By GAROFALO.

1525. STUDY OF A SEATED FIGURE HIS HEAD CLOTHED WITH A TURBAN.
By LORENZO DI CREDI.

1526. STUDIES OF FIGURES AND DRAPERY.

> The centre study at the bottom is for the figure of the Virgin in the Holy Family in the Louvre.

By LIONARDO DA VINCI.

1527. HEAD OF THE VIRGIN.

> Bust to left looking downwards.

By FRA BARTOLOMMEO.   Lent by the MISSES LOUISA AND LUCY COHEN.

1528. SKETCHES OF WOMEN AND CHILDREN.

By LIONARDO DA VINCI.   Lent by SIR FREDERICK LEIGHTON, BART., P.R.A.

1529. THE MARRIAGE OF THE VIRGIN.

> On the back is written : " M. Viasii de gratia ve prego se siati contento de fare ancora uno sposalicio de la madona." Oval composition ; pen and bistre heightened with white. From the collection of J. Richardson, senior.

SCHOOL OF RAPHAEL, ATTRIBUTED TO BIAGIO PUPINI.
                                       Lent by C. FAIRFAX MURRAY, ESQ.

1530. SKETCH.

> A youthful male figure supporting a shell : the legs of another figure seen to the left, and a vase to right ; pen and bistre and red chalk. On the reverse are sketches of figures and ornaments and traces of a head in profile, the last in black chalk. From the Lawrence collection.

By BENVENUTO CELLINI.   Lent by C. FAIRFAX MURRAY, ESQ.

1531. THE FALL OF THE GIANTS.

> Design for a dish. The Gods and Goddesses are seated on either side of Jupiter, who hurls thunderbolts at the prostrate giants ; pen and bistre. On the reverse is a sketch for the stem and handle of a cup and two terminal figures; beneath the foot of the cup, which is ornamented with figures, are the words "tre varie." From the Barnard, Richardson, Cosway, and Lawrence collections.

By BENVENUTO CELLINI.   Lent by C. FAIRFAX MURRAY, ESQ.

1532. THE MARRIAGE OF THE VIRGIN.

> Sketch for the lower part of a composition, engraved by Caraglio ; red chalk, pen and bistre. From the Lawrence and Count de Barck collections.

By PARMIGIANO.   Lent by C. FAIRFAX MURRAY, ESQ.

1533. THE HOLY FAMILY.

> Large Cartoon in charcoal. Virgin three-quarter length seated with the child on her lap, St. Joseph on her left. 34 × 23¾.
> By LIONARDO DA VINCI.   Lent by CHARLES BUTLER, ESQ.

1534. THE JUDGMENT OF PARIS, ST. JEROME WRITING, THE BETRAYAL,

> THE FLAGELLATION, and various emblematical figures and other compositions drawn on six sheets of vellum in pen and bistre ; probably designs for silver work. From the Aylesford Collection.
> FLORENTINE SCHOOL? *c.* 1450.   Lent by C. FAIRFAX MURRAY, ESQ.

1535. STUDY FOR A GROUP IN MICHELANGELO'S LAST JUDGMENT.

> Red and black chalk. From the Russell Collection.
> By DANIELE DI VOLTERRA.   Lent by C. FAIRFAX MURRAY, ESQ.

1536. A YOUNG MAN CONDUCTED AS A PRISONER BEFORE A THRONED FIGURE.

> Three attendants to right and a man on horseback ; bistre heightened with white. From the Crozat, De Tessin, Queen of Sweden, Count Steenborck, and Count De Barck collections.
> By POLIDORO DA CARAVAGGIO.   Lent by C. FAIRFAX MURRAY, ESQ.

1537. THE VIRGIN AND CHILD WITH ST. JOSEPH.

> Portion of a composition of the Adoration of the Kings ; bistre heightened with white on prepared paper. On the reverse is a landscape in water colour. From the Young, Ottley and Bale collections.
> By GIANNICOLA MANNI.   Lent by C. FAIRFAX MURRAY, ESQ.

1538. TWO STUDIES OF AMORINI

> For the pendentive of a vaulted ceiling ; red chalk, pen and bistre. From the Spencer collection.
> By PARMIGIANO.

AND A PANEL OF ORNAMENT FROM THE STECCATA PARMA.

> Pen and bistre, from the Jonathan Richardson, junr., and Barnard collections.
> By PARMIGIANO.   Lent by C. FAIRFAX MURRAY, ESQ.

1539. THE BATTLE OF CASANA, 1364.

Group of nineteen figures; soldiers surprised bathing in various attitudes; a copy in *grisaille* from the famous cartoon commenced by Michelangelo in rivalry of Lionardo da Vinci, for a painting on a wall of the Palazzo Vecchio, Florence, but never carried out; bistre panel 30½ × 51½ in.

After MICHELANGELO.   Lent by the EARL OF LEICESTER.

1540. ST. MICHAEL.

Study for the figure of the Saint in the picture of four Saints with two Angels, in the Academy, Florence. Red chalk. From the Aylesford collection.

By ANDREA DEL SARTO.   Lent by C. FAIRFAX MURRAY, ESQ.

1541. THE MIRACLE OF THE LOAVES AND FISHES.

A circular composition, with numerous figures, pen and bistre wash heightened with white.

By PIERINO DEL VAGA.   Lent by C. FAIRFAX MURRAY, ESQ.

1542. THE ETERNAL.

Seated on the clouds with attendant Angels; design for a lunette; pen and bistre, washed and heightened with white.

By GIULIO ROMANO.   Lent by C. FAIRFAX MURRAY, ESQ.

1543. VENUS.

On a dolphin with two amorini; pen and bistre wash. This drawing has been engraved.

By LUCA CAMBIASO.   Lent by C. FAIRFAX MURRAY, ESQ.

1544. A WATER CARRIER.

Pen and bistre.

By RAPHAEL.   Lent by C. FAIRFAX MURRAY, ESQ.

1545. THE LORD OF THE VINEYARD.

Large crayon drawing of a half-length figure; cross behind; 25½ × 18 in.

By BERNARDINO LUINI.   Lent by HENRY WILLETT, ESQ.

1546. St. John the Evangelist and St. Luke and a High Priest (St. Simeon ?).

Half-length figures, pen and bistre.   Sienese school (?), *c.* 1400.

Lent by C. Fairfax Murray, Esq.

1547. Virgin and Child and St. John.

By Giovanni Antonio Sogliano.   Lent by C. Fairfax Murray, Esq.

1548. Study of a Nude Figure Seated.

By Timoteo della Vite.   Lent by C. Fairfax-Murray, Esq.

1549. Ebony Cabinet Decorated with Figure of Venus and Amorini in Ivory.

Lent by J. Fletcher Moulton, Esq.

1550. Piece of Needlework: The Nativity and the Angels Appearing to the Shepherds.

Lent by Wickham Flower, Esq.

1551. Dixit Dominus.

Within initial letter D.   Christ kneeling in prayer with God the Father ; from a page of Psalter beginning " Dixit Dominus Domino Meo."

Lent by Henry Wagner, Esq.

1552. St. Francis preaching to the Birds.

Within illuminated initial N from the page of a Psalter commencing "Nisi Dominus ædificaverit domum," &c.

Lent by Henry Wagner, Esq.

1553. Virgin and Child.

Small half-length figure of the Virgin holding the Infant Christ.   Gold background. Panel 7 × 5 in.   Painting.

By Pietro da Sano.   Lent by C. P. Rowley, Esq.

1554. Ecce Homo (Pax).

Small half-length figure of Christ standing before the Cross.

Lent by C. P. Rowley, Esq.

1555. BIRTH OF ST. JOHN THE BAPTIST.

Illuminated letter " S," containing in the upper part Elizabeth in bed ; in the lower part the infant John placed in a bath.

Lent by CHARLES BUTLER, ESQ.

1556. BIRTH OF ST. JOHN THE BAPTIST.

Within illuminated initial letter "C."

FLORENTINE SCHOOL.   Lent by EDMUND OLDFIELD, ESQ.

1557. ILLUMINATED PAGE OF A LARGE PSALTER.

(Psalm i.) containing border with large initial " B," within which is a figure of David to whom is appearing God the Father, and below medallions of the Virgin, the Man of Sorrows, and St. John.

Lent by EDMUND OLDFIELD, ESQ.

1558. THE HOLY TRINITY.

Within illuminated letter " B."

By PELLEGRINO DI MARIANO DA SIENA.   Lent by CHARLES BUTLER, ESQ.

1559. TWO APOSTLES.

Within illuminated letter " E."

By PELLEGRINO DI MARIANO DA SIENA.   Lent by CHARLES BUTLER, ESQ.

1560. PORTRAIT OF COSIMO DE' MEDICI (1519–1574).

Bust portrait in profile to right ; red dress and cap ; inscribed on a panel below, "COSMUS MEDICES PATER PATRIÆ." Panel 6½ × 5 in.   From the Magniac Collection.

Son of Giovanni de' Medici, called the Invincible, born 1519 ; called, at the death of Alessandro de' Medici, 1537, to the Lordship of Florence ; received title of Duke from Charles V. ; took that of Grand Duke 1569 ; conquered the territory of Siena and added this to the dominions of his duchy ; died 1574.   He received the title of " Pater Patriæ."

Lent by PERCY MACQUOID, ESQ.

1561. PIETA.

Christ supported by Angels. Panel.

By GIOVANNI BAZZI.   Lent by C. P. ROWLEY, ESQ.

1562. VIRGIN AND CHILD.

Small full-length figures ; the Virgin seated to left on a marble terrace, the Infant Christ on her knees. Landscape background. Panel 11 × 7½ in.

Lent by C. P. ROWLEY, ESQ.

1563. MALE HEAD IN PROFILE

By LIONARDO DA VINCI.   Lent by The REV. W. H. WAYNE.

1564. KNIGHT ON HORSEBACK.

A pen and bistre drawing.

By GIULIO ROMANO.   Lent by The MISSES LOUISA AND LUCY COHEN.

1565. A PROCESSION OF ROMAN CAVALRY.

Crowded scene, spectators on either side. Drawing.

By GIULIO ROMANO.   Lent by HENRY WAGNER, ESQ.

1566. HEAD OF A BEARDED MAN.

Drawing.

By CORREGGIO.   Lent by HENRY WAGNER, ESQ.

1567. THE LAST SUPPER.

Christ seated at a table with the twelve Apostles. Panel 13 × 63½ in.

After LIONARDO DA VINCI.   Lent by C. E. HARRIS, ESQ.

1568. THE ADORATION OF THE MAGI.

Panel.

By BENOZZO GOZZOLI.   Lent by MRS. VIVIAN.

1569. VIRGIN AND CHILD.

Full-length life-size figure of the Virgin, standing towards left in a niche holding The Infant Christ on her right arm. Dated 1491. Fresco, 84 × 37½ in.

Lent by LORD BATTERSEA.

1570. ALTAR PIECE.

In alabaster, with reliefs representing various scenes from the life of the Virgin—the coronation of the Virgin, the Nativity, Christ and the Doctors, the Pentecost, the adoration of the Magi, the Annunciation, Christ appearing to His mother after His death, and the Visitation.

Lent by R. H. BENSON, ESQ.

1571. TABERNACLE.

By LUCA DELLA ROBBIA.   Lent by HENRY WILLETT, ESQ.

1572. DESIGN FOR THE FAÇADE OF THE DUOMO AT FLORENCE, in bistre.

By SANSOVINO.   Lent by MESSRS. DEPREZ & GUTEKUNST.

1573. TWO BACCHANALS.

Sketch in red ware.

By FIAMMINGO.   Lent by J. LUMSDEN PROPERT, ESQ., M.D.

1574. BUST OF A GIRL.

In marble, mounted in a frame.

FLORENTINE SCHOOL.   Lent by W. NEWALL, ESQ.

1575. VIRGIN ADORING THE INFANT CHRIST AND CHERUBIM.

Above, cherubim.   In coloured gesso.

Lent by the DOWAGER COUNTESS OF CRAWFORD.

1576. FRONT OF A CASSONE.

In gesso duro, representing the Judgment of Solomon. $21\frac{1}{2} \times 72$ in.

Lent by CHARLES BUTLER, ESQ.

1577. VIRGIN AND CHILD.

Half-length figures in marble, some parts gilt; in upper portion of the frame a lunette painting of God the Father between two angels.   Dimensions of frame, $51\frac{1}{2} \times 32$ in.

Lent by CHARLES BUTLER, ESQ.

1578. FRONT OF A CASSONE.

Carved in high relief, representing a group of gods and goddesses, amongst whom. are Juno, Venus, Minerva, Mercury, Nymphs, and others. $12\frac{1}{2} \times 57$ in.

Lent by LORD BATTERSEA.

1579. BRONZE CRUCIFIX.

SCHOOL OF GIOVANNI DA BOLOGNA.   Late 16th century.

Lent by MESSRS. DURLACHER BROS.

1580. VIRGIN AND CHILD.

Bas-relief in marble, $25\frac{1}{2} \times 18$ in.

Lent by CHARLES BUTLER, ESQ.

1581. FRONT OF A CASSONE.

Carved in high relief, representing the Rape of Helen.   14¼ × 55 in.

By GIOVANNI DA BOLOGNA.   Lent by CHARLES BUTLER, ESQ.

1582. VIRGIN AND CHILD AND ANGELS.

Coloured bas-relief in gesso duro.   23½ × 21 in.

Lent by the EARL OF WEMYSS.

1583. VIRGIN AND CHILD WITH ST. JOHN.

In gesso duro, coloured.   26 × 17 in.

Lent by W. R. LETHABY, ESQ.

1584. THE ENTOMBMENT.

A coloured group in terra-cotta.

Lent by W. M. CONWAY, ESQ.

1585. THREE BRONZE CLAMPS.

Lent by J. H. FITZHENRY, ESQ.

INDEX OF PAINTERS, SCULPTORS, ENGRAVERS, MEDALLISTS, ETC.

(Under pages.)

N

INDEX OF EXHIBITORS.

(*Under pages.*)

(Under pages.)

www.ingramcontent.com/pod-product-compliance
Lightning Source LLC
Chambersburg PA
CBHW020535270326
41927CB00006B/591